WAUNAKEE PUBLIC LIBRARY
710 SOUTH ST.
WAUNAKEE, WI 53597

What's Doin' the Bloomin'?

A Guide to Wildflowers
of the Upper Great Lakes Regions,
Eastern Canada and Northeastern USA

D0910410

WAUNAKEE PUBLIC LIBRARY
710 ... TH ST
WAUNAKEE, WI 53597

What's Doin' the Bloomin'?

A Guide to Wildflowers
of the Upper Great Lakes Regions,
Eastern Canada and Northeastern USA

Revised & Expanded Third Edition
by Clayton R. Oslund

Thunder Bay Press

Holt, Michigan 48842

What's Doin' the Bloomin'? Revised & Expanded Third Edition
by Clayton R. Oslund

Copyright © 2011 Clayton R. Oslund

All rights reserved

No part of this book may be used or reproduced in any form without writ-
ten permission from the publisher, except in the case of brief quotations
embodied in critical reviews and articles.

Previous editions Published by Plant Pics, LLP

Third Edition published by
Thunder Bay Press
Holt, MI 48842

ISBN: 978-1-933272-22-1

Library of Congress Control Number: 2010940762

About the Cover:
The front and back cover is part of one photograph taken by the author
in Eloise Butler Wildflower Garden, Theodore Wirth Park, Minneapo-
lis, Minnesota. The plant is Yellow Trout Lily *Erythronium americanum,* illustrated on page 14.

Photo Credits:(Photos not listed below were taken by the author).
Wikimedia Commons Photos, GNU Free Documentation License:
James Ellison: p. 43; BerndH: p. 58; Ilona Loser: p.149; Cerceus: p.275; Wal-
ter Siegmund: pp. 125, 254; James Lindsey: p. 268.
Pulic Domain, GNU: pp. 169, 226, 304.
Other Sources:
Hillside Nursery: p. 11; Joshua Horky: pp. 35, 51, 60, 76, 112, 121, 272-273,
279-285, 304.
Charles Peirce: pp. v, 55, 90; Samuel Thayer: pp. 2, 46; Vermont Lady slipper
Co.: p. 41.

Printed in China

Lake Ice Breaking
Spring Flowers will Soon Follow!

Nature's Carpet

State and Provincial Flowers
around
Lakes Huron, Michigan and Superior

from top of page

Michigan
Iris lacustris,
Dwarf Lake Iris

Minnesota
Cypripedium reginae,
Showy Lady's-slipper

Ontario
Trillium grandiflorum,
White or Large-flowered Trillium

Wisconsin
Viola papilionacea
Wood Violet

*To all who have
given encouragement
with each edition
and to those who take time
to enjoy the flowers!*

Acknowledgements

I am especially grateful for the encouragement and assistance of Retta James-Gasser, Naturalist, Gooseberry Falls State Park who was the first person to suggest developing the first edition. She wanted a regional wildflower book with a similar format of the Hawaiian Gardens book my wife and I had just published; pictures big enough to see detail, scientifically accurate without extensive detail, easy to use and interesting to just page through.

All the encouragement and patience from family and friends is treasured! Garden club colleagues, master gardeners and many other groups have continued to embrace the first editions and request presentations for meetings and conferences.

For this third edition, my niece, Rachelle (Shelley) Peterson has been extremely helpful by doing research on the many changes in scientific names, helping to organize and input data and proofreading. Shelley's Mom, my sister Joanne and Husband Dick Peterson have spent many hours proofreading, helping with grammatical detail and giving helpful critique.

A special thanks to my friend, Josh Horky for sharing his collection of native orchid photos which I have developed into a gallery at the end of the book.

Others that have made suggestions and help making decisions on style and presentation include Gordy & Julie, Vince & Ellen, Nick & Julie and Alan who suggested the deer photo be included on page ix.

Then, there has been Kato, my cat that accompanies me, waits on my desk and gives me a few relaxing moments in between times!

"Let's Get to Work. . .
We have a Book to Write"!
Kato

Just Looking!

. . . an observant passer by.

Wildflower Watching

Tips on Using This Book

Spring, Summer, Fall: Following the Pattern

Plants come and grow about the same time each season. For this reason, they are grouped by their bloom time, beginning with early spring flora. Changes in environment may cause plants to flower days earlier or be delayed. Once in bloom, some plants have flowers that last only a few days, while others display their flowers until frost-killed in late fall.

The first five sections contain herbaceous plants, arranged in a pattern from early spring continuing into autumn . Each of the next four sections, Vines, Trees & Shrubs, Grasses & Sedges, and Ferns, Club mosses and Horsetails are also organized by season. This pattern will not always be an accurate indication of the sequence of beginning bloom time because species vary a great deal on length of time they continue to bloom.

Familiar Faces

It's easy to remember a face and forget the name! With the sequence pattern in mind, use this guide to find a photo of a plant you recognize. Next, page through other pictures in that time-frame. The plant in question may be at your fingertips.

Companion Guides

No single book is complete: Every region has a unique plant population. Other books, based on keys and line drawings, may help to identify unknown plants. The author suggests Newcomb's Wildflower Guide, listed in the bibliography, as a useful companion to this book. For more detail, the book by Gleason and Cronquist along with its illustrated companion by Holmgren are very useful.

Discover Characteristics of Plant Families

Check out the information given about naming plants on page xi and in the Plant Family Facts section on pages 286-290.

Taking Notes

Most pages have a small space for jotting down a note. For example, information on date, where seen, or other plants in the same location may help you remember where to find a favorite wild flower in the future.

Plant Names 101

Plant names are often thought to be difficult. This is due in part to the thousands of plants we encounter in many aspects of life. We learn plant names to identify fruits and vegetables in our gardens and grocery stores. There are multitudes of trees, shrubs, flowering perennials, annuals and some plants we designate as weeds in our fields, pastures, lawns and gardens, and they all have names. When we come to parks, forests and other natural areas there are more species!

Grouping plants helps the recognition process. At the grocery produce department, let's consider some lettuces: Head, bib, cos, romaine, and leaf lettuce are a few examples in the "lettuce group." Among other flowering plants in the garden, we may have planted several kinds of lilies including Asiatic, Day, Oriental, Tiger and Wood Lilies. Each group (Lettuce or Lily) is a collection of individual types that have characteristics in common.

Plants have common and scientific (botanical or Latin) names. Using the lily group as an example, "Wood Lily" is a common name and *Lilium philadelphicum* the scientific name for one individual type. Each individual plant type has a genus and species name; *Lilium* is the genus and *philadelphicum* the species name.

Major changes have taken place recently due primarily to the ability to use DNA analysis.

Family names are based primarily on flower and fruit structure. Other factors such as stem, leaf or root characteristics also give clues to grouping plants into families. A summary of plant families presented in this book is found on pages 286 to 290.

Scientific or botanical family names have an *aceae* (pronounced like the letters of the alphabet A-C-E) ending. *Liliaceae* is an example of the scientific family name for the group of plants we call lilies. Other names may not be so obvious, such as those of the Potato Family, also called Tomato, Nightshade or Tobacco Family. All of these belong to the *Solanaceae* Family. *Solanum tuberosum* is the genus and species name for "potato" in the *Solanaceae* Family. This sorting out of plants illustrates the need for scientific names. Often several common names are applied to one group of plants which can certainly become confusing.

Nature's Handiwork

Table of Contents

Where to Find Them

EARLY SPRING IN JAY COOKE STATE PARK, MINNESOTA

Come, join me on a wildflower walk!

Looking down in Jay Cooke! It isn't necessary to go far to please the eyes. More to come as we move through the seasons.

Spring Beauty
Claytonia virginica (right)
Claytonia caroliniana (below*)*
Portulacaceae (**Purslane**) **Family**

There are two very similar species of Spring Beauty. The major difference is in the leaves with **C. virginica** (right) having narrow, linear leaves and **C. caroliniana** (below) having broader leaves. Flowers of both, borne on short, weak stems, show colors that may be shaded from white to pink.

Moist woodlands are common habitat. After blooming, leaves die down and disappear by mid-summer.

Spring Beauty in the Garden

Believe it or not ~ Spring Beauty, in addition to being lovely to look at, can be eaten! These tiny plants develop tubers about 2 to 3 inches deep which may grow up to 1.5 inches in diameter. They have been referred to as "fairy spuds".

Ref: Samuel Thayer has an interesting commentary on using Spring Beauty tubers in his book "The Forager's Harvest." It is included on a list of recommended references on page 300

Spring Beauty tubers

Samuel Thayer

Bloodroot
Sanguinaria canadensis
Papaveraceae (Poppy) Family

The clump above and enlarged inset is a form that has more than 4 petals. Not common, but do occur in natural habitats.

Normal Bloodroot (flowers left) have 4 white sepals and 4 white petals. Sepals are slightly larger than petals.

Note two leaves clasping the flower pedicle (stalk) on this double Bloodroot (above) This is a rare natural variation that has been propagated commercially. These double flowers last longer that normal single flowers. It cannot produce seed as the reproductive parts have all become modified into petals. It is referred to as:

Sanguinaria canadensis 'Multiplex.'

Bloodroot capsules develop under the canopy of leaves. Inset shows the white eliasome which is sweet, attracting ants which carry the seeds away to their nest. After eating the eliasome the seed is able to germinate and produce a new plant.

Bloodroot in the Garden

Either the single or double bloodroot is a good plant for naturalizing in a shade garden landscape.

Single flowered types are easy to propagate from seed if seeds are gathered fresh and planted before they dry out. If the seed dries, germination may be delayed for a year or the seed may die. Seeds could be stored moist and refrigerated for a few months before planting. Germination should then occur.

Rhizomes (photo below) form branches and dividing them is a quick way to start a new garden or expand your bloodroot patch.

Bellwort or Merrybells
Uvularia grandiflora

Bellwort grows to about 12 to 18 inches tall. It typically looks wilted while leaves are expanding and while it is blooming. After blooming, leaves and stems become more erect and take on an appearance similar to Solomon's-seal.

Wild Oats or
Sessile Bellwort
Uvularia sessilifolia

Wild Oats (right is shorter, only 6 to 12 inches in height. Flowers are smaller, creamy colored and have more blunt tips on the petals than *U. grandiflora*.

A Name Change
Uvularia species are in *Colchicaceae*; formerly classification was *Liliaceae* (Lily) Family

Bellworts in the Garden

U. grandiflora is a very nice perennial for landscaping. It is easy to grow and brings a rich yellow color to early spring landscapes before most other perennials start blooming. Leaf texture is an added attraction all summer long.

Widely available in native plant nurseries as bare root divisions, one division will grow into a clump ready to be divided again in 1 to 3 years.

Trailing Arbutus bloom season is early and short. Flowers are very fragrant. Its usual habitat is dry Pine forests.

Sadly Trailing Arbutus are becoming very hard to find because the plant is so sensitive to being disturbed such as when woodlands are logged or even when blossoms are picked.

Trailing Arbutus
Epigaea repens
Ericaceae (**Heath**) **Family**

Dutchman's-breeches
Dicentra cucullaria
Fumariaceae (**Bleeding Heart**) **Family**

Delicate flowers are very short lived. To catch a glimpse of this delightful plant, it is necessary to keep a vigil in early spring. The flower shape is a clue on what led to its name "Dutchman's-breeches."

This is a true ephemeral. All traces of the plant disappear after flowering and seed production. They can be grown in the home garden, but it is easy to lose them unless they are well marked.

Liverleaf or *Hepatica*
Hepatica nobilis var. *obtusa*
Hepatica nobilis var. *acuta*
Ranunculaceae (Buttercup) Family

Hepatica nobilis var. *acuta* leaves

A Name Change

Liverleaf is commonly referred to by its scientific name, ***Hepatica***. A recent name change has put both types into one species rather than two. These two varieties differ primarily by the shape of their leaves. Variety ***obtusa*** (formerly ***H. americana***) has round lobes, and var. ***acuta*** (formerly ***H. acutiloba***) has pointed lobes. ***Hepatica*** come in a range of colors; white, blue, violet and pink.

Hepatica in the Garden

An excellent choice to complement a garden in shade, especially under deciduous trees. The following characteristics apply to Hepatica:

*Early show of color in the spring.

*Leaves stay green throughout the summer for a pleasant ground cover.

*Easy to propagate; have a fibrous root system so can be divided when the clump enlarges.

*Readily available at specialty wildflower nurseries.

*Grow well in any good garden soil.

Hepatica nobilis var. *obtusa* leaves

White and Pink *Hepatica nobilis* flowers

Hepatica are among the early spring ephemerals (plants that have flowers lasting only a few days or even just one day).

Leaves may overwinter, turning a rusty brown color, or be packed down by snow, causing the flowers to poke up through fallen tree leaves. New green leaves soon appear after flowers have faded.

Flowers appear to have 6 to 10 petal-like colored sepals (the first ring or whorl of parts on a flower). Many species of the Buttercup Family have flowers with colored sepals but no petals.

Pale lavender *Hepatica nobilis* flowers come out early spring. New leaves are beginning to develop in this clump.

Snow or
Dwarf White Trillium
Trillium nivale

This is the smallest Trillium and the earliest to bloom. It is a rare find as the northern most range, according to the USDA maps, is the Green Bay area of Wisconsin.

7

Skunk Cabbage
Symplocarpus foetidus
Araceae (**Arum**) **Family**

Skunk Cabbage is one of the earliest spring flowers. As soon as water logged marshes (where it grows abundantly) thaw out in the spring, the plant sends up its mottled spathes (leaf-like coverings) which surround the spadix (floral spike). Jack-in-the-Pulpit (page 20) and Wild Calla (page 28) are other examples of spathe and spadix.

The flowers inside are visible for just a short while, and the spathes soon become hidden by large leaves, which resemble cabbage, as pictured below.

The name "Skunk Cabbage" comes from the unmistakable odor of "skunk" when the leaves are crushed.

Nearly black fruits which resemble pineapples in shape develop and become exposed late in the season when autumn frosts kill the leaves.

Fruits

Flowers

Wild Ginger
Asarum canadense
Aristolochiaceae (Birthwort) Family

Large, heart-shaped leaves help make Wild Ginger easy to identify in its woodland habitat. It prefers soils rich in nutrients.

Its unusual flowers are quite inconspicuous at the base of the plant and can be observed only by pushing the leaves aside.

These gingers are not the source of the "spice" ginger which comes from an unrelated plant in the **Zingiberaceae** (Ginger) Family grown in tropical climates.

Wild Ginger in the Garden
Wild Ginger is often used as a ground cover in shady home gardens. This and several other ginger species (non native, but hardy to regions of zone 4 or 5) are commercially propagated and available at many garden centers and mail-order nurseries.

Large-flowered or White Trillium
Trillium grandiflorum

Where found: Woodlands across south shores of Great lakes. Abundant south of Duluth, but scarce along the North Shore of Lake Superior.

The Trillium Family: A Name Change

This gets to be a long story. Most references place Trillium in *Liliaceae* (Lily) family. More recently it has been placed in the *Melanthiaceae* family. Some authors use *Trilliaceae* which had been used since 1846 giving Trillium their own special family. Most authors in that time period maintained *Liliaceae* as the name. However, in 2003, the international group of systemic botanists established *Melanthiaceae* as the official name! (ref. Wikipedia)

Large-flowered Trillium is also called Large-white Trillium. By whatever name, the flowers turn shades of pink as they finish blooming and wither. Large-flowered Trillium has three broad leaves that remain throughout summer and are held on a stem about 12 to 18 inches tall. Although flowers may vary in size, they all bloom above the leaves.

This is Ontario's Provincial flower.

Nodding Trillium
Trillium cernuum

Nodding Trillium flowers typically hang down under three broad leaves which are similar in shape to the leaves of **T. grandiflorum**. White flower petals curve backwards. Pink stamens are another identifying characteristic. Fleshy, bright-red berries usually develop after flowers fade. The yellow flower in the photo is Bluebead; described on the next page.

Double Trillium
T. grandiflorum 'Flore Pleno'

A double flowered form rarely occurs naturally. However, when it does, and then propagated vegetatively, specialty nurseries may propagate it to offer as a horticultural cultivar.

Hillside Nursery

Trillium in the Garden

Shade gardening with native plants is becoming a popular practice, especially with many of these woodland wildflowers being introduced to the nursery trade by new propagating techniques or by being salvaged from wild areas designated to be destroyed by road building or commercial developments.

Several species of Trillium are now available from specialized nurseries and are useful in home landscapes as companions to Hosta, ferns, and other shade tolerant plants.

More on pages 7, 37.

11

Bluebead
Clintonia borealis
Liliaceae (Lily) Family

Bluebead is easy to recognize in the fall. Its brilliant blue fruit is an absolute give-away. Such brilliant blue is not common in fruits and flowers. The berries are reported to be mildly toxic.

In some areas it is known as Corn Lily due to leaves that resemble corn.

When the broad leaves come up early in the spring, surrounding the flower stalk, and may be confused with Wild Leek (page 46). Unlike leek, Bluebead leaves remain green most of the summer.

Distinctive yellow flowers bloom on a slender stalk and clearly identify this as Bluebead.

Cutleaf Toothwort
Cardamine concatenata
Brassicaceae (Mustard) Family

Toothworts grow 6-12 inches. A flower stem is topped in a cluster of small, four-petaled pink or white flowers. Terminal clusters of flowers are on an erect stem with deeply cleft leaves. They stand above a whorl of basal leaves that are deeply divided and coarsely toothed.

Two-leaved Toothwort has only two nearly opposite, deeply dissected stem leaves, each with three toothed lobes. Toothworts bloom in the spring; the common name refers to the tooth-like projections on underground stems.

A Name Change
Still in the Mustard family, but note change in genus. Cutleaf Toothwort species is now ***Cardimine concatenata*** rather than ***Dentaria laciniata*** and Two-leaved Toothwort is now ***Cardamine diphylla*** rather than ***Dentaria diphylla.***

Two-leaved Toothwort
Cardamine diphylla
Brassicaceae (Mustard) Family

Toothwort in the Garden
Its easiest to start plants from pieces of the rhizome. These should be planted a little below the surface of the ground in an area with sparse ground cover that receives shade during the summer. Spring planting is recommended. Cutleaf Toothwort develops quickly and is one of the earlier spring wildflowers of woodlands. The foliage turns yellow and fades away by the end of spring. This plant typically grows in dappled sunlight before the trees leaf out. It prefers moist to mesic conditions and a rich loamy soil with decaying leaves.

Yellow Trout Lily
Erythronium americanum

These early spring plants pop up in thick masses, each with one flower stalk sandwiched between two leaves. Once it has flowered and produced seeds, the entire plant disappears by early summer.

Trout Lilies are also called Dog Tooth Violets or Adder's Tongue.

Trout Lilys are in
Liliaceae (Lily) **Family**

White Trout Lily
Erythronium albidum

In the garden

Trout lilies thrive in a loamy garden soil which is not subject to being disturbed. They give a quick show in early spring and self propagate to increase the size of the bed.

Being planted along with later emerging and blooming wildflowers works very well.

Wood Strawberry
Fragaria vesca
Rosaceae (Rose) Family

Similar at first glance, Wood Strawberry has seeds (actually achenes which contain the seeds) on the surface of the berry while Common Strawberry (below) has achenes imbedded in pits within the red receptacle that makes up the strawberry fruit. The leaves of *F. vesca* are somewhat more pointed than in *F. virginiana*.

In the garden
Common wild strawberries are a connoisseurs delight! In cultivation, they become more robust than when competing with other plants in the wild.

Common Strawberry
Fragaria virginiana
Rosaceae (Rose) Family

15

Early Meadow Rue
Thalictrum dioicum
Ranunculaceae
(Buttercup) Family

Flowers of Early Meadow Rue dangle from the upper portion of the plant like miniature decorative ornaments shimmering in the breezes. Yellow anthers are the most conspicuous part of these tiny flowers.

Miterwort or Bishops Cap
Mitella diphylla
Saxifragaceae
(Saxifrage) Family

Miterwort is also called Bishop's Cap, a name derived from the shape of the flower. Tiny flowers (inset) with five delicate fringes have a dainty appearance. Uppermost leaves are opposite and sessile (not having stalks or petioles). Slightly lobed, heart-shaped basal leaves have petioles. The leaf in the lower right corner of the photo is not Miterwort but is Large-leaved Aster (page 196) which is commonly found in the same habitat.

More wildflower garden choices
Both of these species readily adapt to a light to moderately shaded area with good garden soil. Miterwort is easy to propagate from seed which germinates immediately upon dispersal.

Wild Lily-of-the-Valley
Maianthemum canadense
Ruscaceae Family

Wild Lily-of-the-Valley (sometimes called Canada Mayflower) typically has two leaves (occasionally three). The flower has four radiating points, an identifying characteristic.

Three-leaved False Solomon's-seal, a confusing look-alike, *Maianthemum trifolia*, always has six points to its flower and normally has three leaves (page 63).

Name Changes

Maianthemum genus is now in *Ruscaceae* formerly in *Liliaceae*. Also brought into *Ruscaceae* are *Smilacina* (False Solomon's-seals) and *Polygonatum* (Solomon's-seals).

In the Garden

Wild Lily of the Valley can be naturalized in most garden soils and tolerate heavier shade than most other wildflowers.

Fruits of Wild Lily-of-the-Valley begin to develop shortly after flowering, first becoming white berries mottled with small red spots, becoming all red by fall.

17

Dog Violet
Viola conspersa

Violaceae (Violet) Family
There are over 80 species reported in North America, and differences in species are subtle, often difficult to identify.

Several species of violets have prominent spurs protruding from the base of the lower petal. Dog Violet has a somewhat blunt spur. Its leaves are broad and heart-shaped. Long Spurred Violets boast a more slender spur.

Violets in the Garden
Violets are drought tolerant but also thrive in moist soil habitats. My garden has violets of all colors which have appeared naturally. They do not seem to be invasive, but provide a nice natural companion to other ornamental plants.

Long Spurred Violet
Viola selkirkii

Marsh Marigold
Caltha palustris

Marsh Marigold is often found growing in shallow water ditches, quiet lake shores and ponds or wet, marshy areas.

Each flower bears multiple seed capsules with many seeds which are quickly released.

Marsh Marigold in the garden

Marsh Marigold, like many other native plants, are used in woodland landscaping and can tolerate soils that are not soggy wet.

This plant is easily propagated as the seed germinates immediatly upon dispersal. Therefor one must watch for the capsules to open, then collect the seed and plant immediately.

Caltha and *Copis* are in *Ranunculaceae* (Buttercup) Family.

Goldthread
Coptis trifolia

Goldthread forms a rosette of shiny, 3-lobed, compound, evergreen leaves. Flower stalks arise 3 to 6 inches from the base of the rosette and form single white flowers with 4 to 7 petaloid sepals early in the spring. It grows in cold, damp woodlands or bogs.

The name Goldthread is derived from a yellowish-orange colored rhizome growing just below the soil surface.

Jack-in-the-Pulpit
Arisaema triphyllum
Araceae (Arum) Family

The Arum Family has an unusual flower arrangement. Tiny, almost inconspicuous, flowers are borne on a pencil-like stalk called the spadix. The spadix is surrounded by a sheath called a spathe. In Jack-in-the-Pulpit, the spathe bends forward nearly hiding the flowers on the spadix inside.

There are variations in the color of the spathe from plant to plant. It may be green or have purplish stripes. Some authors separate the variants into three different species.

The fanciful spring spathe disappears when clusters of bright green berries form on the spadix in summer. By fall the berries turn bright red. Each berry has one or more seeds.

Wild Calla (page 28) and Skunk Cabbage (page 8) are other examples of plants in the Arum Family.

Jacks in the garden

Jack-in-the-Pulpit is easy to grow. Flowers areinteresting and it's fruit cluster is colorful in the fall. Ripe berries can be collected and buried in soil and seeds should germinate come spring. There is a faster way to start plants. I have an article on *Arisaema* propagation for the Wild One's Journal (publication date unknown prior to printing this book) See page 302.

Wood Violet
Viola papilionacea

Blue is the predominant color in violets. Downy Blue Violet is identified by a white throat and "beards" on the two side petals which extend into the white throat. Purple stripes accent the lower petal. There are fewer species of yellow and white violets within the scope of the Great Lakes region in comparison with the blues. **This is Wisconsin's State Flower.**

Downy Yellow Violet
Viola pubescens

Downy Yellow Violet has broad heart-shaped leaves that are fuzzy on the underside. The flower stalks arise along the stem and are short and fuzzy. ***Viola rotundifolia*** or Roundleaf Yellow Violet (not pictured) has flowers that arise from the base of the plant. It is native to the northeastern area covered by this book.

Canada Violet
Viola canadensis

Canada Violet is a common white violet. A light-purplish tinge on the back of the upper two petals will identify ***V. canadensis***. Its flower stalks originate on the stem. Also native to the region are ***V. renifolia*** and ***V. blanda***.

Red Baneberry
Actaea rubra

Baneberrys grow from 1 to 2 feet tall and produce either red or white berries in the fall. Both types bloom with white flowers. White Baneberry has a slightly elongated flower cluster while Red Baneberrys have a more rounded cluster.

Both plants are reported to be poisonous, however, Naegele in *Edible and Medicinal Plants of the Great Lakes Region* reports that he has "eaten the berries without feeling ill effects." He notes that "the berries are so bitter, it is improbable that anyone would eat more than one."

Actaea species are in Ranunculaceae the Buttercup Family

Red Baneberry (white form)
Actaea rubra alba

Baneberry in Woodsy Landscapes
When several are planted close together, they appear to clump as one large, showy, "shrub-like" plant in the summertime. The leaves stay green and the fruits are showy in autumn.
Nurseries which supply perennials often offer Baneberry. They can also be started from seed, however, the seed usually does not emerge until the second year after planting.

Doll Eyes or White Baneberry
Actaea pachypoda

The name "Doll Eyes" comes from the black spot on the end of the shiny, white berry. The thick red pedicles holding the white berry distinguishes this plant from the white form of **A. rubra**.

Moschatel or Muskroot
Adoxa moschatellina
Adoxaceae
(Moschatel) Family

Cradled in the exposed root of a Cedar tree, this Moschatel seems to flourish. It is a rare and endangered species making it difficult to find. It grows only 2 to 4 inches tall. In springtime it produces a pale greenish yellow flower followed by a small berry.

Golden Alexanders
Zizia aurea
Apiaceae (Parsley) Family

Golden Alexanders resembles Wild Parsnip (page 124). A look at the leaves shows that they are doubly compound leaves with each of 3 leaflets divided again 3 to 7 times. Wild Parsnip has leaves divided into 5 to 15 leaflets that are not further subdivided.

Full sun in a meadow as well as shade at the forest's edge can be habitat for Golden Alexanders. It often shares it's woodland habitat with ferns. Here it is accompanied by Maidenhair fern **Adiantum pedatum** (page 266).

In the garden
Golden Alexanders is a biennial. It can be started from seed or transplants.

Along the edge of a woodland garden makes a good habitat.

Smooth Rock Cress (left)
Arabis laevigata

Smooth Rock Cress grows 1 to 3 feet in height. Basal leaves are somewhat lobed and upper linear leaves have small lobes that clasp the stem.

Arabis species are in *Brassicaceae* (Mustard) Family.

These are biennial plants producing large amounts of seed.

Lyre-leaved Rock Cress
Arabis lyrata

Lyre-leaved Rock Cress is a delicate, weak-stemmed plant about 5 to 10 inches tall. The basal leaves are deeply lobed (see inset), while the leaves on the upper stem are small and linear.

25

Wild Sarsaparilla
Aralia nudicaulis

Aralia and *Panax* **species** are in *Araliaceae,* the **Ginseng Family.**

Sarsaparilla sends up a leaf stalk from a rhizome (underground stem). Shortly afterward, a stalk bearing 3 or 4 round clusters of greenish-white flowers appears. As the summer progresses, blue-black berries develop (right).

Its large, spicy-aromatic rhizome can be collected in the fall. An extract from this plant, along with others in the ginseng family, has been

used as an ingredient in making root beer or a tea for medicinal purposes. The sarsaparilla extract of commerce for making root beer actually comes from a tropical species of Greenbrier (*Smilax*), page 216.

Dwarf Ginseng
Panax trifolius

Dwarf Ginseng has three compound leaves each of which may have 3 to 5 leaflets. Note the 3 large and 2 small leaflets.

Similar to Ginseng used as an herbal remedy (opposite page), this dwarf form, only 4 to 8 inches tall, is found in nutrient-rich soils of moist wooded areas.

A rounded umbel begins to develop as a tight cluster of buds (below). With lengthening of the flower stalk, the umbel expands into a delicate cluster of white flowers. Yellow berries develop later.

Ginseng
Panax quinquefoliuis

Ginseng begins its spring growth with an inconspicuous round cluster of yellow-green flowers blooming on short stalks at the terminal point of the stem similar to those of Dwarf Ginseng.

Three long stalked leaves, each with 5 leaflets, also arise from the same terminal point.

Berries turn bright red in late summer and remain upright in the center of the three leaves.

Wild Ginseng has become a cultivated crop primarily for herbal remedies and is quite rare in its natural habitats.

Spikenard
Aralia racemosa

Spikenard stems grow 3 to 6 feet tall and have large, spreading compound leaves with many oval leaflets. It grows well in humus-rich woodlands.

Clusters of purple berries develop from hardly noticeable greenish-white flowers.

Aralia in the Garden
Spikenard makes a good "edge of the woods" plant in the landscape. It is available in nurseries devoted to wildflower propagation.

Wild Calla
Calla palustris
Araceae (**Arum**) **Family**

Wild Calla is usually found growing in shallow water, in bogs, or edges of ponds or lakes. The pure white spathe surrounds a golden colored spadix which produces a cluster of small green fruits (see arrow in lower photo) that turn red later in the season.

In the Garden
Wild Calla is easily grown in a shallow pond.

False Rue Anemone also lacks petals, having 5 showy white petaloid sepals. The leaves are similar to Rue Anemone and other **Thalictrum** in appearance. (**Thalictrum**, pages 16 and 71). A tell-tail difference is in number of colored sepals. While False Rue Anemone has 5, Rue Anemone may have 5 to 10 petaloid sepals. Rue Anemone (below) flowers range from pink to white. Rue Anemone is found in more southerly regions.

False Rue Anemone
Enemion biternatum
SYN: *Isopyrum biternatum*

All Anemones are in **Ranunculaceae** (Buttercup) Family

Anemones in the Garden
False and true Rue Anemones are especially attractive in a woodland garden. Several colors and forms of the **T. thalictroides** are available in nurseries listed on page 301.

Rue Anemone (below)
Thalictrum thalictroides

Wood Anemone (left)
Anemone quinquefolia
Wood Anemone blankets the forest floor in localized areas. It is one of several flowers that is referred to as "Mayflower." Flowers are usually white, but may be tinged with pink. Being in the Buttercup Family, the showy Anemone flower parts are sepals as is the case with Hepatica on pages 6-7.

Rose Twisted Stalk
Streptopus lanceolatus var. *roseus*
Liliaceae (Lily) Family

A zig-zag stem suggests the name Twisted Stalk. Its leaves resemble those of Solomon's-seal (page 79) and False Solomon's-seal (page 75). Branching stems are a typical growth pattern.

An abundance of mottled-rose, bell-shaped flowers arise from the base of the leaves. Bright red berries develop, but soon drop off or are eaten by critters of the forest.

White Mandarin or Twisted Stalk
Streptopus amplexifolius
Liliaceae (Lily) Family

Larger than Rose Twisted Stalk (facing page), White Mandarin has a similar structure. A major identifying characteristic is the twisted pedicle (flower stalk) shown left. Flowers are creamy-white to green. Red fruits develop in mid- to late summer. Fine hairs on the lower stem, shown in the lower right photo, are another clue to its identity.

May Apple or Mandrake
Podophyllum peltatum
Berberidaceae (Barberry) Family

Each May Apple plant has only one white pendulous flower extending from the crotch of two large leaves. The flower produces one large berry 1 to 2 inches long. Fruit ripens to yellow and is edible fresh. Please take caution with the rest of the plant as the resins are toxic.

The name Mandrake has been applied to May Apple, but the historical Mandrake is *Mandragora*, in the *Solanaceae* family, and was grown for medicinal purposes generations ago. *Mandragora* root was thought to mimic human form. According to the "Doctrine of Signatures," the root was useful in curing disease or treating a part of the human body that it resembled.

Mandragora species are native to the Mediterranean and Himalaya regions.

A favorite of shade gardeners
May Apples grow well in heavily shaded areas and naturalize easily. They are available from specialty nurseries.

Early spring growth

Swamp Saxifrage
Saxifraga pensylvanica
Saxifragaceae (**Saxafrage**) **Family**

A whorl of oval, blunt leaves at its base is a good clue to the identity of this plant. Flower stalks develop which sometimes grow to be over three feet tall. Flowers may vary from the cream color shown here to white or even a light shade of purple.

33

Field Pussytoes
Antennaria neglecta
Asteraceae (Aster) Family

Pussytoes are woolly plants that have mostly leafless scapes (flower stalks) and are usually less than 12 inches tall. There are several species which are difficult to distinguish without technical expertise.

Some authors call Pussytoes "Everlastings." Another plant Anaphalis margaritacea (Pearly Everlasting) has flowers similar to Pussytoes but grows taller (page 165).

Male and female flowers are produced on separate plants with most plants being female. Seeds will form even though the female flower is not pollinated (parthenogenesis).

Pistillate flowers

Female or pistillate plants

Male (staminate)

Mature wind-blown seeds

Mat of leaves after flowering

Elegant Groundsel
Packera indecora
Asteraceae (Aster) Family

Elegant Groundsel is quiet rare. It is native to the boreal regions of Northeastern Minnesota, Michigan's upper peninsula, Wisconsin's rocky Lake Superior shore line and Ontario. This photo was taken on a rocky cliff along Lake Superior.

Early Sweet Coltsfoot
Petasites palmatus
Asteraceae (Aster) Family

Growing in well-drained but wet soil, Early Sweet Coltsfoot produces a flower shoot up to 2 feet tall from an underground stem before leaves appear. The flower stalk has leaf-like bracts. Male and female flowers are found on separate plants.

After blooming, basal leaves (left) appear which are 4 to 6 inches in diameter and have 5 to 7 deeply cut lobes.

Wood Betony or Lousewort
Pedicularis canadensis
Orobanchaceae (Broomrape) Family

A sturdy low-growing plant up to 12 inches tall, its stem and leaves are hairy (pubescent). Notice the deeply lobed, lance-shaped leaves. Dense clusters of yellow (or sometimes reddish) flowers bloom their way up the flower stalk over a period of 2 to 3 weeks. Its habitat is dry, open woods.

"Lousewort" is a name that translates as louse plant. It is applied to about 30 species of *Pedicularis*. According to folklore, it was believed that cattle and sheep would get lice when they came into contact with the plants.

Name Change

Pedicularis was previously listed in *Scrophulariaceae* (Snapdragon) Family. The change reflects its hemiparasitic character. As it grows along with other plants, such as grass as shown in the photo, it attaches to the grass plant and may draw water and other nutrients from it. Another hemiparasitic plant is Indian Paintbrush (page 60).

Purple or Red Trillium
Trillium erectum
Melanthiaceae (Name change see page 10)

Later blooming than other Trilliums common to the area (pages 7, 10-11), Purple Trillium grows up to 2 feet tall. Even though the species name, **T. erectum**, would seem to indicate that the flowers stand erect, they more often appear to droop as seen below.

White to cream colored flowers are variations within the species.

Purple Trillium may be found in more southerly parts of the Great Lakes region.

Trillium in the Garden

Trillium are usually started in the garden using dormant rhizomes. Because Trillium begin their growth very early in spring, fall is the best time of the year to plant. Unless the rhizome has been kept cold over winter, it will begin to form a shoot before being able to plant in spring. Note the bud on the rhizome pictured (left). This is in perfect condition for planting. Four to six inches is the proper depth.

Blue Cohosh
Caulophyllum thalictroides
Berberidaceae (**Barberry**) **Family**

Initial springtime growth emerges as a deep purple shoot. Leaves soon turn green followed by greenish-yellow flowers. Bright blue fruits develop in late summer. Blue Cohosh is much easier to recognize in the fall.

Although the fruits resemble "blueberries" (page 228), Cohosh berries are toxic. Blue Cohosh grows in moist, nutrient rich woodlands, reaching heights of 1 to 3 feet.

Virginia Waterleaf
Hydrophyllum virginianum
Hydrophyllaceae (Waterleaf) Family

Leaves of Virginia Waterleaf are often mottled with irregular white spots, giving the appearance of being water stained. Pale-lavender, bell-shaped flowers hang in clusters. Stamens protruding beyond the petals give the flowers a "whiskery" look.

This woodland plant thrives in shade conditions, especially when the soil is moist and humus rich.

Blue Cohosh and Waterleaf
in the Garden

Both of these plants make interesting additions to a woodland garden. The unique purple color of the Blue Cohosh in the spring is always an "eye-catcher".

The soft appearance of Waterleaf flowers is very attractive. In addition, the first leaves in spring have small white patches scattered on the upper surface. A few spring leaves are visible in the lower right corner of the picture.

Spreading Dogbane
Apocynum androsaemifolium
Apocynaceae (**Dogbane**) **Family**

A shrubby-looking herba-
ceous perennial growing up
to 4 feet tall, Spreading Dogbane shows off spring-time
finery with bell-like, pink-
striped blossoms.

Its stems are reddish-brown
and contain a milky sap. This
sap may cause dermatitis.

Large Yellow Lady's-slipper
Cypripedium parviflorum var. *pubescens*
Orchidaceae (Orchid) Family

Yellow Lady's-slipper is one of the more common orchids across the region. It is usually found in hardwood forests but also grows in swampy areas and meadow-like habitats. There are two variations of *Cypripedium paviflorum*; var. *pubescens,* the Large Yellow Lady's-slipper, and var. *makasin* or Small Yellow Lady's-slipper. Variety *makasin* differs by having a smaller pouch and darker red petals and sepals.

C. makasin

Vermont Ladyslipper Company

41

Showy Lady's-slipper
Cypripedium reginae
Orchidaceae (Orchid) Family

Adapted to a wide range of habitats, the Showy Lady's Slippers can be found in coniferous and hardwood swamps and wet meadows. It is also found in roadside ditches that have been undisturbed for many years, growing in direct sunlight. Being a long-lived plant, it produces a larger clump each year. **This is Minnesota's State Flower.**

Lady's-slippers in the Garden
Native Lady's-slippers are a delight to have in the shady landscape. In recent years a method of producing them by laboratory methods has made them readily available for home planting.

Both the Showy and White Showy are available from several sources. (See list of nurseries on page 301).

These nurseries supply planting instructions to insure success for long lasting enjoyment. The photos on this page were taken in the author's yard.

White Showy Lady's-slipper
Cypripedium reginae
var. *albolabium*

A rare albino or white form.

Pink Lady's-slipper or Moccasin-flower
Cypripedium acaule

One of the most common of the temperate climate slipper orchids, look for it in shaded habitats from dry sandy forests to wet bogs and swamps. These habitats are usually acidic.

Sometimes called Stemless Lady's-slipper, this plant has a long flower stalk which comes up between two basal leaves growing from the crown of the plant.

Hardy Orchid Trivia

Orchid fruit is a dry capsule (left) which is filled with dust-like seed. Typical of orchids, these seeds do not have an endosperm or food reserve. To germinate and grow, the seed needs to have a partnership with a fungus in the soil that provides food while the young plant is developing. Several years of underground development may take place before the orchid sends shoots above ground

By supplying the needed nutrients in a test tube culture media, the association with a fungus is circumvented. This makes it possible to have nursery propagated plants.

Moccasin Flowers in the Garden

The secret of success with *C. acaule* is to make sure the soil is acidic. When these are planted in a garden, it is necessary to maintain an acid soil condition.

Ram's-head Lady's-slipper
Cypripedium arietinum

Ram's-head Lady's-slippers are very rare in Minnesota and Wisconsin. It is on their threatened species lists. It is more prevalent in Upper Michigan and the Northern part of the Lower peninsula.

Being a small plant, it is difficult to find even if one is in the area. It has been found in a range of habitats, including coniferous and deciduous forests and sphagnum bogs.

James Ellison

Spotted Coral Root
Corallorhiza maculata
Orchidaceae (Orchid) Family

Striped Coral Root
Corallorhiza striata

What, no green leaves? Most orchids have green leaves to conduct photosynthesis, but ***Corallorhiza*** species rely on a symbiotic relationship with a fungus for all their nourishment, not just during embryonic development, but during the entire life of the plant! The fungus gets its nourishment from digesting decaying organic material in the soil. In an intimate relationship with the orchid's roots or rhizome, the fungus transfers the nourishment to the orchid.

Spotted Coral Root is widely distributed through out northeastern U. S. and southeastern Canada. Another ***Corallorhiza*** ,***C. trifida,*** Early Coral Root is in the Orchid Gallery on page 285. A more mature ***C. striata*** is pictured on page 284

Spotted Coral Root

Buckbean
Menyanthes trifoliata
Menyanthaceae
(Buckbean) Family

Name change
Formerly, *Meyanthes* was
included in *Gentianaceae*
(Gentian) Family.

Common to Sphagnum peat bogs,
muddy lake shores and shallow water
ponds, Buckbean exhibits its lovely
cluster of white blossoms held above
three large, oval-shaped leaves. These
leaves only resemble those of the
common garden beans and are in no
way related to the Legumes.

Buckbean in the Garden
The flowers tend to be long-
lived making it a good candidate for a bog garden. Both
seeds and plants are available
at specialty nurseries.

Wild Leek or Ramp
Allium tricoccum
Liliaceae (Lily) Family

Wild Leek first appears in the spring with two broad basal leaves. As the flowers begin to open, the leaves wither. Only shriveled remnants are left behind.

Samuel Thayer provided the photo of bulbs harvested to be used in cooking. Mr. Thayer's book "The Forager's harvest" (ref. p. 300) details the identification, harvesting and use of many other native plants as food.

Leeks, in genus **Allium** along with onions and garlic, are listed as being in **Amaryllidaceae** (Amaryllis Family) according to some references.

Early Spring Leaves

Leek bulbs

Developing inflorescence

Inflorescence

Fruit cluster

Yellow Iris
Iris pseudacorus
Iridaceae (Iris) Family

Now found in marshes and wet roadsides, Yellow Iris has escaped from home gardens.

It is a **European native** that has become naturalized. It is also regularly sold in garden centers for home landscaping.

Yellow Water Buttercup
Ranunculus flabellaris
Ranunculaceae
(Buttercup) Family

Characteristic to this aquatic species, most of Yellow Water Buttercup's finely divided leaves are submerged. Leaves that are above water are less divided. Small yellow flowers are held above the water's surface. Quiet water of ponds or bays is the usual habitat.

Another name given to this species is Yellow Water-crowfoot.

White Pea
or Pale Vetchling
Lathyrus ochroleucus
Fabaceae
(Pea or Legume) Family

Creamy-white flowers and compound leaves, usually with 6 egg-shaped leaflets, identify White Pea. Tendrils are found at the tip of the leaves.

Small-flowered Crowfoot
Ranunculus abortivus
Rununculaceae
(Buttercup) Family

Tiny yellow petals and sepals surround a green button-like cluster of reproductive parts at the center of the Crowfoot flower.

The "crowfoot" leaves are on the upper part of the stem. Roundish, toothed leaves are found at the base of the plant. Small-flowered Crowfoot may grow up to 24 inches tall but is often as short as 6 inches.

Purple or Water Avens
Geum rivale
Rosaceae (Rose) Family

Nodding flowers with purplish sepals and yellow petals hang atop long stems that have small leaves divided into 3 segments. Basal leaves have 3 large segments at the tip with several smaller leaflets along the rachis (midrib).

Purple Avens in the Garden

Purple Avens prefers a moist, highly organic soil. While partial shade is desirable, especially at mid-day, they will withstand full sun if the soil remains moderately moist.

A nice feature is a long bloom period followed by attractive fruiting heads which stand upright rather than drooping as do the flowers while in bloom.

49

Star Flower
Trientalis borealis
Primulaceae (Primula) Family

At the top of a short, sturdy stem, Star Flower has a whorl of 5 to 10 leaves and two star-like white flowers blooming at the center.

Count the petals. (Normally there are seven!) Few plant species have flower parts in multiples of seven, making Star Flower a rarity.

Golden Ragwort
Senecio aureus
Asteraceae (Aster) Family

Golden Ragwort is characterized by a flat-topped flower cluster, finely cut upper leaves, and rounded leaves at its base. Growing 1 to 3 feet tall, its common habitat is wet meadows and swampy areas.

Virginia Bluebells
Mertensia virginica
Boraginaceae (Borage) Family

Tall or Northern Bluebells
Mertensia paniculata
Boraginaceae (Borage) Family

Joshua Horky

Blooming takes place over a prolonged period from spring to early summer in Virginia Bluebells. Flower color changes from pink when in bud to blue when fully open.

Egg-shaped leaves are alternately arranged on a stem growing 1 to 2 feet tall. Once flowering is over, the leaves wither and disappear.

Northern Bluebells differs by having dangling flowers. Leaves stay green all summer as well. In fact, it is somewhat invasive.

Virginia Bluebells in the Garden

Virginia Bluebells works very well with perennials that get a slow start in springtime. When the Bluebells have finished blooming and the shoots have gone dormant, other perennials may take their place.

These plants are readily available as dormant rhizomes, some suppliers sell seed, or you may collect your own. The seed should not dry out, but can be stored cold in moist vermiculite.

51

Winter Cress
Rorippa spp.
Brassicaceae (**Mustard**) **Family**

This and other Cresses are examples of Mustard Family plants that "pop up" in many places as weeds, especially common in agricultural crops. Carried by birds and other means, mustard seeds are spread throughout the region. These Cresses are **introduced species** from around the world.

Sheep, Field or Common Sorrel
Rumex acetosella
Polygonaceae
(Buckwheat) Family

Sheep Sorrel is a wide-spread plant of **European origin**. It has become naturalized throughout the region and is a **persistent weed** in many fields and gardens. It spreads by rhizomes and by seeds and grows in wet as well as dry soils, in nutrient rich soil as well as poor.

Attractive, spear-shaped leaves have flaring lobes at their base. Sheep Sorrel, with its reddish inflorescence, makes a dramatic appearance as ground cover.

Common Groundsel
Senecio vulgaris
Asteraceae (Aster) Family

Common Groundsel has golden-yellow flowers in heads that do not fully open. Bracts surrounding the flower heads have black tips. Flowers continue to bloom throughout the summer, producing multiple generations of seeds in one season. Leaves are long and deeply lobed.

Native to Europe, it has naturalized throughout the Great Lakes region and has become a **tenacious weed**.

53

Thimbleweed
Anemone virginiana
Ranunculaceae
(Buttercup) Family

Thimbleweed is also called Tall Anemone. It grows to up to 3 feet in height. Flower centers appear as "buttons" which stretch as they develop into "thimbles." Each long flower stalk supports one flower made up of 5 white petal-like sepals.

Lupine
Lupinus perennis
Fabaceae
(Pea or Legume) Family

Lupinus perennis is our native Lupine. It is found in open areas in habitat illustrated by the photo. Regions a few counties away from the upper Great Lakes may be the best area to search.

Most blue, pink, and white Lupines we see in more northerly areas around the Great Lakes in dry meadows and roadsides are *Lupinus polyphyllus,* western states natives or hybrids escaped from gardens.

©Charles peirce

Wild Columbine
Aquilegia canadensis
Ranunculaceae
(Buttercup) Family

Columbines are distinctive with long spurs extending backward on their petals. The sepals in Wild Columbine are red and showy, extending forward between each of the petals which are yellow and blunt in front.

Habitats of Wild Columbine range from woods to open meadows and as landscape plants in home gardens.

"Domestic" columbines constitute a wide collection of other species and hybrids. Plants with large blooms in many color choices are now available commercially.

56

Wild Geranium
or Spotted Cranesbill
Geranium maculatum
Geraniaceae (Geranium) Family

Wild Geranium, a common woodland plant, grows up to 2 feet high.

Seed capsules (left) illustrate the "Cranesbill" shape which gives the plant its name. The seeds are in the "knob" (or carpel) at the end of the curls. Each flower has 3 to 5 of these curls that pop free from the capsule to disperse the seed.

Cranesbill in the Garden

Along with several other *Geranium* species and hybrid cultivars, it has been domesticated for home gardens.

Butterwort
Pinguicula vulgaris
Lentibulariaceae
(Bladderwort) Family

Thriving in the same habitat as Bird's-eye Primrose, these tiny Butterwort plants trap insects! Its curled leaf is the natural appearance. A slimy covering, feeling "greasy" to touch, attracts and traps small insects. The leaves then roll up and digest the insects. Bon appetit! The flower is similar to that of a violet.

Shade has Come to the Forest

Bird's-eye Primrose
Primula mistassinica
Primulaceae (Primrose) Family

Bird's-eye Primrose is a general name for primroses that have the yellow "eye." ***P. mistassinica*** is also called Dwarf Canadian Primrose. It is characteristically only a few inches high and commonly grows in cracks among rocks as seen below. These were found on a rocky, north shore cliff of Lake Superior.

59

Indian Paintbrush or Painted Cup
Castilleja coccinea
Orobanchaceae
(Broomrape) Family

Name change

The genus and species name have not changed, but the family name has changed from *Scrophulariaceae* (Snapdragon) Family. The major consideration is the hemiparasitic characteristic as with Wood Betony (page 36).

Strikingly beautiful, often seen in a meadow or open woods, the Indian Paintbrush shows off its brightly colored bracts. Orange-red is the most common color, but occasionally a plant with yellow bracts may be found. Greenish-yellow flowers are inconspicuous, remaining nearly hidden by the bracts. It grows 1 to 2 feet tall and has forked leaves along a single stem.

Indian Paintbrush is a hemiparasite. This means that it is parasitic under natural conditions and also carries out photosynthesis to some degree. The host plant may just be a source of water and mineral nutrients or may supply some organic nutrients as well.

Joshua Horky

Hoary Puccoon
Lithospermum canescens
Boraginaceae
(Forget-me-not) Family

This herbaceous perennial is found in dry, open or wooded areas. Its rich, golden color is especially eye-catching on roadsides. Stems grow 12 to 18 inches tall, and like the rest of the plant, are covered with fine hairs.

A name given by the Indians, "puccoon" relates to red dye which can be extracted from the roots.

Shepherd's Purse
Capsella bursa-pastoris
Brassicaceae (Mustard) Family

Shepherd's Purse is another **European introduction** now naturalized in North America. In addition to being found in open woods and native meadows, it is a persistent weed in fields and gardens. The name comes from the shape of the dry, triangular fruits resembling a pouch or bag used by a shepherd.

61

Caraway
Carum carvi
Apiaceae (**Parsley**) **Family**

Fine-textured leaves and dainty white flowers in a small umbel characterize Caraway.

Aromatic seeds are used as seasoning in many foods, especially rye bread and cabbage dishes.

A **native of Eurasia**, Caraway has escaped from cultivation and now is found growing in road ditches and other dry, open places.

Three-leaved False Soloman's-seal
Maianthemum trifolium
Ruscaceae (Ruscus) Family

Maianthemum genus is now in *Ruscaceae* formly in *Liliaceae*. Also brought into *Ruscaceae* are other False Solomon's-seals and *Polygonatum* (Solomon's-seals).

Three-leaved False Soloman's-seal is similar to Wild Lily-of-the-Valley or Canada Mayflower (page 17). The six petals, best indicated in the photo by the shadow of the flower within the yellow circle, differentiate it from Mayflower, which has 4 petals.

Swamp Buttercup
Ranunculus septentrionalis

Swamp Buttercup differs from Tall Buttercup (opposite page) by having compound leaves with short stalks on the leaflets. The rounded leaves under the compound leaves in the photo above are Marsh Marigold leaves.

As the name indicates, Swamp Buttercup thrives in wet woods and meadows, growing to about 3 feet tall.

Anemone and *Ranunculus* are in *Ranunculaceae (Buttercup)* Family

Canada Anemone
Anemone canadensis

One of the most common Anemones, it spreads by long underground stems, often producing large patches once it gets established. Compare Wood Anemone (page 29) which is shorter and earlier blooming.

Canada Anemone favors damp woods and meadows and grows to about 18 inches tall. Compound leaves are stalkless.

Tall or Common Buttercup
Ranunculus acris
Ranunculaceae (Buttercup) Family

Growing to 3 feet tall, this Buttercup has showy golden-yellow flowers with overlapping petals. The stem is usually hairy. Lower leaves are deeply cut into several lobes and are larger than those higher on the stem.

Open forests and meadows are common habitat.

Lesser Stitchwort
Stellaria graminea
Caryophyllaceae
(Pink) Family

Dainty white flowers appear to hang in mid-air on thin stems, a typical growth pattern of Lesser Stitchwort.

Belonging to the Pink Family, it has 5 petals that are cleft or partially divided, some cleft so deeply that it may look like 10 petals rather than 5 (photo lower right).

Bright rusty red anthers stand out against the snow white petals. It is an alien species that has become naturalized and is quite common in grassy places.

Grove Sandwort
Moehringia lateriflora
Caryophyllaceae
(Pink) Family

Grove Sandwort has been moved out of the genus *Arenaria* to *Moehringia*.

Grove Sandwort is a low-growing perennial that thrives in open wooded areas. Fragile-looking stems may support one or more flowers.

These plants spread by underground rhizomes, forming a patch.

The photo below shows Grove Sandwort growing along with Wild Lily-of-the-Valley (page 17).

Orange Hawkweed
Hieracium aurantiacum
Asteraceae (Aster) Family

A **European native**, Orange Hawk-weed has spread throughout our region. It establishes itself quickly by stolons and forms dense mats. The leaves and stems are fuzzy. Unopened buds (right) have a deep purplish-black appearance.

Often mistaken for Indian Paintbrush (page 60)

Smooth Hawkweed
or Glaucous King Devil
Hieracium piloselloides
Asteraceae (Aster) Family

Another **European native**. This Hawkweed has a rosette of basal leaves that have fine hairs along the edges. Flowers form on branching clusters atop a nearly leafless stem.

Like most Hawkweeds, this species is prolific and grows abundantly, thriving in sunny locations along roadsides and open fields.

H. piloselloides is also referred to as ***H. florentinum*** in earlier references.

Common Milkweed
Asclepias syriaca.
Asclepiadaceae (Milkweed) Family

Clusters of pink flowers give way to large milk-weed seedpods. Packed inside the pad are seeds topped with tufts of silky hairs. Once the pod splits open, the tufted seeds become scattered with the wind.

Milkweed leaves are the favorite food of Monarch butterfly larvae. This black and yellow caterpillar eats its way across the leaves, while the plant seems oblivious to its role in the life cycle of the butterfly.

Purple Meadow Rue
Thalictrum dasycarpum
Ranunculaceae (Buttercup) Family

Purple Meadow Rue grows to 5 feet tall on distinctively purple stems. Sometimes it is called Tall Meadow Rue.

Dangling flowers on the Purple Meadow Rue have white sepals, no petals and greenish-yellow stamens.

Beach Pea
Lathyrus japonicus
Fabaceae (Pea or Legume) Family

Found on sandy shores of the Great Lakes, eye-catching bicolored flowers stand out against its lush green foliage. Compound leaves have broad leaflets and large arrow-shaped stipules.

Black Snakeroot
or Maryland Sanicle
Sanicula marilandica
Apiaceae (Parsley) Family

At first count, Black Snakeroot often appears to have 7 leaflets on the larger compound leaves. A closer look reveals that the side leaflets are cleft so deeply they each appear as two rather than one.

Flowers are greenish-white and form bristly burs with hooks.

Starry False Solomon's-seal
Smilacina stellata
Ruscaceae Family

Red berries develop in autumn.

Starry False Solomon's-seal is a miniature of its taller relative, ***Smilacina racemosa*** (opposite page). Tolerating a wide range of habitats, Starry False Solomon's-seal thrives on sunny sand dunes of the Great Lakes to shaded, nutrient rich woodlands. These durable little plants become a striking ground cover in nature.

False Solomon's-seals in the Garden
Smilacina racemosa is used in home landscaping in woodland settings. It compares with ***Polygonatums***, true Soloman's Seal, as a landscape plant.
S. stellata, however, is very invasive and will soon take over a garden plot. It does work well as a groundcover where there is room for expanding growth.

False Solomon's-seal
Smilacina racemosa
Ruscaceae Family

Smilacina, False Solomon's-seal's genus, is now in *Ruscaceae* formly in *Liliaceae*. Also brought into *Ruscaceae* are *Polygonatum* and *Maianthemum* genera (pp. 17, 79).

False Solomon's-seal can be recognized by the cluster of white flowers at the tip of the stem. Fruits from these flowers become bright red in autumn.

Leaves and stem are look-alikes to true Solomon's-seal (page 79). Habitat of each of these species is similar. Light shade of woodlands with nutrient rich soil is ideal for them to flourish.

Prairie Plantain
Plantago patagonica
Plantaginaceae (Plantain) Family

Prairie Plantain is found in open, dry, sandy shores of the Great Lakes regions. It grows to about 6 inches in height. Flowers are borne in silky, pubescent spikes. Leaves are covered with fine hairs. Prairie Plantain looks "woolly."

Prairie Smoke
Geum triflorum
Rosaceae (Rose) Family

Altough being a prairie plant, Prairie Smoke is found in patches in the openings among the woodlands in the Great Lakes regions. While it prefers full sun, it is slightly shade tolerant and can grow in sandy or loam soil. A cluster of hairs 1-3 inches long, is responsible for the alternate name of Old-man's Whiskers.

Prairie Smoke In the Garden

Many homes in the region have praire-like conditions and Prairie Smoke can make a nice addition of color and texture in the garden. Easy to grow along with other sun or light shade tolerant perennials.

Bird's-foot Trefoil
Lotus corniculatus
Fabaceae
(Pea or Legume) Family

Bird's-foot Trefoil is a handsome plant with showy yellow flowers that give way to slender seed pods. These pods look like a bird's foot, hence its name. It is a **native of Europe** that has naturalized in North America. Compound leaves have 5 leaflets, the lower two similar to stipules.

Cardinal Flower
Lobelia Cardinalis
Campanulaceae
(Bellflower) Family

Cardinal flower is found in the more easterly regions covered by this book. Closer to Lake Michigan and East. Although native there, it is used as a landscape plant throughout the region.

In the Garden
It's natural habitat is in wet areas. However it does well in a garden soil with consistent moisture.

False Heather (below)
Hudsonia tomentosa
Cistaceae (Rockrose) Family

False Heather mimics the scale-like leaves of true Heathers. With its natural ground-cover tendency, it grows into thick, shrubby mats about 8 inches deep. Bright yellow flowers form at the tips of the twigs.

Its habitat is the dry, sandy beaches and dunes of the Great Lakes.

Mouse-eared Chickweed
Cerastium vulgatum
Caryophyllaceae (Pink) Family

Mouse-eared Chickweed has hairy stems. Flower petals have a typical cleft, trademark of the Pink Family. It can be a pesty weed in lawns and gardens as it spreads quickly once established.

Both of the plants on this page are **introduced species,** and have invaded and become naturalized.

Black Medic
Medicago lupulina
Fabaceae (Legume) Family

Black Medic has a sprawling growth habit. Yellow flowers form a tight cluster followed by black, coiled seed pods. Once established on roadsides, waste places, lawns and gardens it becomes an invasive weed.

Solomon's-seal
Polygonatum biflorum
Ruscaceae Family

Great Solomon's-seal has flower clusters of two to several per node. **P. biflorum** usually has only two flowers per node. **P. commutatum** is reported to be a tetraploid, having twice the number of chromosomes as **P. biflorum**.

Some authors prefer to list these variants as a single species, **P. biflorum**.

Great Solomon's-seal
Polygonatum commutatum
Ruscaceae Family

Rough Cinquefoil
Potentilla norvegica
Rosaceae (Rose) Family

Identifying characteristics include a hairy stem, compound leaves with 3 leaflets (most cinquefoils have 5 - 7 leaflets), and green sepals extending out longer than the bright yellow petals. These tenacious plants may blossom when only a few inches tall or grow to 3 feet in height.

Norwegian Cinquefoil is another name for this plant. Although it bears a Norwegian name, it is native to the US and Canada.

Wood Sorrel
Oxalis stricta
Oxalidaceae
(Wood-sorrel) Family

Wood Sorrel leaves are compound with 3 heart-shaped leaflets resembling clover leaves. These are sometimes called Sour Clover due to the taste of high oxalic acid content in the leaves.

It is widespread on roadsides, open places, and areas of disturbed soil. There are several other species of Wood Sorrels including *O. violacea* (not pictured) with pink-purple flowers.

O. stricta is listed as native in the US, but non-native to Canada according to the USDA profile.

Forget-me-not
Myosotis scorpioides
Boraginaceae (Forget-me-not) Family

Yellow-eyed, bright blue flowers bloom on masses of deep green foliage, thriving on wet soils and even in shallow water.

Of **European origin**, it has escaped from gardens to become established in many different regions.

81

Purple or American Vetch
Vicia americana
Fabaceae
(Pea or Legume) Family

Purple Vetch typically has an open or loose cluster of flowers on a smooth stem that climbs by tendrils at the leaf tips. Leaflets are narrow and oblong. Look for a toothed stipule at the base of the leaves.

Long-leaved Bluet
Houstonia longifolia
Rubiaceae (Bedstraw) Family

Bluet plants usually form clumps in dry, open wooded or rocky areas.

Clusters of white to light lavender flowers bloom on the stem tips.

Dame's Rocket
Hesperis matronalis
Brassicaceae
(Mustard) Family

Similar to garden Phlox in color and form, Dame's Rocket deserves to be recognized on its own merits. Being in the Mustard Family, the flowers have 4 petals. It also has a pleasant fragrance. Phlox has 5 petals and little fragrance.

It is **not native** to North America.

Bugle
Ajuga reptans
Lamiaceae (Mint) Family

Bugle is a mat-forming plant about 8 inches high that spreads by leafy stolons. Now widely used in shade gardens as a ground cover, Bugle shows off its handsome leaves and lovely spring flowers. **Brought over from Europe**, it is another garden escapee, naturalizing throughout the region.

Ajuga is sometimes called Bugleweed, but another mint family plant, ***Lycopus uniflorus*** (page 213) is recognized as Bugleweed.

Twinleaf
Jeffersonia diphylla
Berberidaceae
(Barberry) Family

The range of Twinleaf extends into more southerly regions covered by this book.

With its attractive foliage and eye-catching white flower, this woodland plant becomes a welcome addition to shade garden landscapes. It is now propagated and available in specialty nurseries.

As green fruits develop (below), leaves continue to elongate, covering up the fruit completely by late summer. Note inset with mature capsule and seeds.

Twinleaf in the Garden

With the appealing early flower, followed by curious fruiting capsules becoming covered by butterfly shaped wings, Twinleaf makes an interesting addition to a woodland garden.

Three-toothed Cinquefoil
Sibbaldiopsis tridentata
Syn: *Potentilla tridentata*

Both of these Cinquefoils thrive on the rocky cliffs of Lake Superior's North Shore. Three-toothed Cinquefoil is recognized by compound leaves with 3 leaflets, each having 3 small "teeth" at the tip.

Three-toothed Cinquefoil in the Garden
This attractive plant is at home in a rock garden setting, with ample moisture.

These two Cinquifoils are *Rosaceae* (Rose) Family plants

Silvery Cinquefoil
Potentilla argentea

Silvery Cinquefoil leaves are deep green with white, woolly undersides. Each leaf has deeply cut lobes giving it an appearance of a small oak leaf. Stems are fuzzy, too. This a non-native species of **Eurasian origin**.

Blue Phlox
Phlox divaricata
Polemoniaceae (Phlox) Family

Wild Blue Phlox In the Garden
Wild Blue Phlox is often used in home landscaping to naturalize an area. It is available from specialty nurseries. Another name commonly given to this plant is Woodland Phlox.

Gill-over-the-ground
Glechoma hederacea
Lamiaceae (Mint) Family

Also called Creeping Charlie or Ground Ivy, Gill-over-the-Ground is a notorious weed. It has become a bane to homeowners whose lawns and gardens are in somewhat shaded areas. Another **Eurasian species**, it is naturalized throughout the Great Lakes Region and beyond. To its credit, the blue blossoms are quite pretty.

Yellow Corydalis
Corydalis flavula
Fumariaceae
(Bleeding Heart)Family

Yellow Corydalis is another woodland perennial that has found its way into gardeners' landscapes. With lovely lacy foliage, this plant stays attractive right through the summer. Yellow Coydalis purchased at a nursery will usually be a **European** species, *C. lutea*, which has larger flowers.

Another Corydalis, *C. aurea* or Golden Corydalis, is also found in this area. It takes a trained eye to distinguish a difference in the flowers. *C. flavula* has a small toothed crest on the upper petal and a shorter spur than *C. aurea*. Pale Corydalis with a pink flower (page 204) blooms later in the season.

Hooker's Orchid
Platanthera hookeri
Orchidaceae (Orchid) Family

Name
Hooker's Orchid may be listed in the Genus *Habenaria* by other authors. Smith, in *Orchids of Minnesota*, reports that the current trend is to place terrestrial orchids, previously included in *Habenaria,* into the *Platanthera* genus. Other Orchids in this genus include *P. ciliaris* (page 139), *P. hyperborea* (page 120) and *P. psycodes* on page 140.

Upland pine forests are a common habitat for Hooker's Orchid, but it has been found in deciduous forests as well. The yellowish-green flowers bloom on a stalk about 8 to 15 inches tall.

Check out the Orchid Gallery on pages 279 - 285

Twinflower
Linnaea borealis
Caprifoliaceae
   (**Honeysuckle**) **Family**

In the same pine forests that are home to Hooker's Orchid, Twinflower flourishes. These dainty bell-shaped blossoms come in pairs on a single slender stalk. The plants have a trailing habit, spreading into colonies.

This is the only species in Genus *Linnaea*.

Blue Flag
Iris versicolor
Iridaceae (Iris) Family

Widely distributed throughout the region, Blue Flag fills the marshes and roadside ditches with dashes of color.

Dwarf Lake Iris
Iris lacustris
Iridaceae (Iris) Family

Dwarf Blue Iris has limited distribution. **It is the state Wildflower of Michigan.** It is on the threatened species list in Michigan. Michigan also has a state flower, the Apple Blossom.

©Charles peirce

Poison Ivy
Toxicodendron radicans
Anacardiaceae
(Sumac or Cashew) Family
Syn: *Rhus radicas*

Flower buds developing

Spring flowers

ALL PARTS POISONOUS!

Overwintered berries in spring

First season berries

Bird-on-the-wing
or Gaywing
Polygala paucifolia
Polygalaceae (Milkwort) Family

Another denizen of pine forests, Bird-on-the-wing is named for the fanciful flowers which have the appearance of two birds flying in opposite directions. The quaint flowers may look orchid-like, but the plant is not an orchid.

Partridge Berry
Mitchella repens
Rubiaceae
(Madder) Family

Partridge Berry is a creeping plant that takes root at the nodes of the stem forming a large mat. Nearly round, shiny green leaves with a greenish white strip on the midrib are identifying features. White flowers with 4 petals form in 2 flower clusters at the end of a stem.

The fruit is a bright red berry.

Greenish-flowered Pyrola
Pyrola virens
Ericaceae (Heath) Family

Pink Pyrola
Pyrola asarifolia
Ericaceae (Heath) Family

Name Change

Pyrola species were traditionally in *Pyrolaceae* (**Wintergreen**) **Family.** New molecular studies indicate a closer relationship to *Ericaceae* (Heath) Family.

Pictured here are two examples of *Pyrola* species. Others have white flowers, one of which is later blooming and pictured on page 158. Pyrolas are found growing in pine forests among mosses and through pine needle mulch on the forest floor.

Purple Pea
Lathyrus venosus
Fabaceae
(Pea or Legume) Family

Similar to Beach Pea in color and form of plant (page 72), Purple Pea has flower clusters that are elongated and crowded with more blossoms.

Purple Pea is better adapted to a wider range of habitats, especially to wooded areas with light shade.

Northern Bedstraw
Galium boreale
Rubiaceae (Bedstraw) Family

Northern Bedstraw has smooth, erect stems up to 2 feet tall. Narrow linear leaves are in whorls of 4 compared to other Bedstraws that have 6 leaves in a whorl (Rough Bedstraw, page 147). Flowers in tight clusters are abundant.

Wood Lily
Lilium philadelphicum
Liliaceae (Lily) Family

Vibrant orange petals stretch upward on Wood Lily. Lance-shaped leaves are in whorls on the upper part of the stem but opposite on the lower stem. Meadows and open woods are ideal habitats.

Bastard Toadflax
Comandra umbellata
Santalaceae (Sandalwood) Family

Meadows, prairies and open woods are also ideal habitats for Bastard Toadflax. Being in the Sandalwood Family, it follows the trait of attaching its roots to the roots of another plant in order to draw nutrients from its host. Even though it uses this parasitic attribute, Bastard Toadflax has chlorophyll, producing some of its own food as evidenced by its green leaves.

Honewort
Cryptotaenia canadensis
Apiaceae (**Parsley**) **Family**

A typical characteristic of Honewort is the unequal length of the rays of the umbel. Each small cluster of flowers has a stalk of varying length. It has a compound leaf with each leaflet showing a different lobe pattern.

One-flowered Wintergreen
Moneses uniflora
Ericaceae (**Heath**) **Family**

Name Change
Like the *Pyrola, Moneses* has been reclassified from the **Wintergreen Family** *(Pyrolaceae)* to the **Heath Family.**

Also called Wood Nymph, this miniature plant is only 2 to 5 inches tall. It has a rosette of evergreen leaves at the base of the flower stalk. Each plant supports one flower. Common habitat is coniferous woodlands. Also found in Cedar bogs.

97

Pitcher-plant
Sarracenia purpurea
Sarraceniaceae (**Pitcher-plant**) **Family**

Sphagnum peat bogs are common habitat for insect-eating Pitcher-plants.

A rosette of pitcher-shaped leaves at the base are partly filled with water. Insects make their way inside where they are trapped, digested and absorbed, providing nourishment to the plant. This is important source of nitrogen from the protein of the insects.

Dragon's-mouth
Arethusa bulbosa
Orchidaceae (Orchid) Family

Dragon's-mouth typically grows in Sphagnum bogs. It usually appears to be leafless while flowering. It is rare to find a specimen with a leaf and flower. More often than not, the flower has withered before a single grass-like leaf appears. The species name **bulbosa** refers to its bulb-like corm.

Note the **Scouring Rush** or *Equisetum* parallel to the Orchid (see page 275).

Cow Parsnip
Heracleum maximum
Apiaceae (Parsley) Family

This giant herb may grow up to 8 feet and sometimes taller. Umbels of elegant white flowers in flat clusters bloom at the top of the plant. Compound leaves have 3 deeply-toothed leaflets. Its hollow stem is up to 2 inches in diameter.

Water Hemlock
Cicuta maculata
Apiaceae (Parsley) Family

Water Hemlock, a plant of wet ditches, swamps and meadows, grows from 3 to 6 feet tall. It is recognizable by its compound leaves with narrow lance-shaped, toothed leaflets. Some of the leaflets are twice or thrice compound. A hollow branching stem has streaks of purple.

CAUTION: The fleshy taproot is highly poisonous. It has been fatal to persons who have eaten it. Water Hemlock is similar to Water Parsnip, ***Sium suave***, a non-toxic plant (not pictured).

Bicknell's Cranesbill
Geranium bicknellii
Geraniaceae (Geranium) Family

Deeply-cut, lobed leaves and sprawling manner give a
delicate air to this Geranium. It has loose clusters of small
pink to light lavender flowers. This is a native plant that
becomes a weed in many gardens.

Large-flowered Beardtongue
Penstemon grandiflorus
Plantaginaceae (Plantain) Family

Large-flowered Beardtongue likes sandy prairies, but it will take up residence in prairie-like habitats in the westerly and southerly Great Lakes regions. Beautiful flowers present themselves at the top of the stem. This perennial grows from 2 to 3 feet tall.

"Beardtongue" describes one of 5 stamens which is sterile (not producing pollen). In some species, this special stamen is covered with hairs (bearded).

Pineapple Weed
Matricaria discoidea
Asteraceae (Aster) Family

Although native to Western North America, it has spread throughout the eastern regions becoming a prolific weed, especially unwanted in gardens.

Stems and leaves are aromatic, smelling like pineapple when crushed.

Flower heads are unusual by having only central disk flowers without showy ray flowers like daisies or asters.

103

Western Jacob's-Ladder
Polemonium occidentale
Polemoniaceae (Phlox) Family

Western Jacob's-Ladder is a rare find in the Great Lakes area. According to USDA records it can be found in only one county in Minnesota (St. Louis) and one county in Wisconsin (Florence) east of the mountain states. This photo was taken in a cedar swamp in Itasca county Minnesota

The Pacific coastal and Mountain states comprise the largest population.

Cow or Tufted Vetch
Vicia cracca
Fabaceae (Pea or Legume) Family

Tufted Vetch, of **Eurasian origin**, is naturalized throughout this region, especially along roadsides and meadows. The plant is weak-stemmed and sprawling. Compound leaves are long with up to 10 narrow leaflets terminating in a tendril. Its inflorescence is long and one-sided having as many as 30 flowers.

Yellow Goat's Beard
Tragopogon dubius
Asteraceae (Aster) Family

Also called Western Salsify, this plant looks like a giant Dandelion especially when the large, yellow flowers turn into fluffy, 3 to 4 inch diameter globe-shaped seed heads. Like Dandelion seed, the wind scatters Yellow Goat's Beard to new locations.

Heal-all or Selfheal
Prunella vulgaris
Lamiaceae (Mint) Family

This native plant easily invades lawns, fields and roadsides with its spreading growth habit. Violet flowers are produced in dense heads. As its name suggests, it is still used as an herbal medicine.

Ox-eye Daisy
Leucanthemum vulgare
Asteraceae (Aster) Family

Ox-eye Daisy establishes itself in meadows, roadsides and lawns, spreading by rootstocks and self-seeding. It is often seen in large patches or throughout an entire field. Left on its own, it may grow up to 3 feet tall.

It is not native to North America, but has been introduced from Eurasian sources and is considered a noxious weed.

"Fresh as a Daisy" Ox-eyes and Heal-all bloom through the transition of late spring into summer.

Alfalfa or Lucerne
Medicago sativa

Alfalfa, an **Asian native**, is another cultivated plant for pasture and hay production throughout this region. It grows in clumps up to 3 feet tall. Purple to blue-violet flowers change into a spiral pod which has up to 3 full turns. Like other perennial field crops, Alfalfa is also widely naturalized.

Alfalfa and all Clovers are in *Fabaceae* (Pea or Legume) Family

Red Clover
Trifolium pratense

Red Clover, **native to Europe**, is widely cultivated as a pasture or hay crop and has also escaped cultivation to become naturalized. The magenta flowers are in compact round heads. Oval leaves usually show a pattern of white in the shape of a V.

Alsike Clover
Trifolium hybridum

Alsike and White Clovers, like Red Clover, are cultivated plants of **Eurasian origin**, now widely distributed and naturalized.

These two clovers have similar flower heads. To tell them apart:

(1) White Clover has a pale, greenish-white crescent on its leaflets. Alsike leaflets are solid green.

(2) White Clover flower stalks and leaves grow up from creeping runners. Flowers and leaves of Alsike come from branching stems.

White Clover
Trifolium repens

Yellow Sweet Clover
Melilotus officinalis

Sweet Clovers are in *Fabaceae* (Pea or Legume) Family

Sweet Clovers, Yellow and White, are coarse-stemmed clovers used for hay and pasture. Because of their deep roots and nitrogen fixing process, both of these species produce a large amount of biomass, growing 2 to 4 feet tall. They are used for soil building by plowing them down as a "green fertilizer" crop.

White Sweet Clover
Melilotus albus

Valerian or Garden Heliotrope
Valeriana officinalis
Valerianaceae
(Valerian) Family

Growing 2 to 3 feet tall, Valerian is topped with a compact cluster of white to pinkish flowers. In late summer, spent flowers drop off leaving behind a lacy-looking red residue (photo bottom left). Leaves are deeply divided into lance-shaped segments.

111

Greater Bladderwort
Utricularia vulgaris
Lentibulariaceae
     (Bladderwort) Family

Underwater leaves have tiny "bladders" that trap and digest minute aquatic organisms as their food source. Flower stalks emerge above the water producing clusters of two-lipped yellow flowers. Quiet ponds or ditches with a continuous water supply are home to this water plant.

Lavender Bladderwort
Utricularia resupinata

Joshua Horky

Narrow-leaved Cattail
Typha angustifolia
Typhaceae (Cattail) Family

Common Cattail
Typha latifolia
Typhaceae (Cattail) Family

Cattails are well-known plants of marshes and wet ditches. Two similar species can be identified quickly by a difference in their flower spikes. Male and female flowers of Narrow-leaved Cattail are separated by a gap (see arrow). Each Cattail has male flowers on the upper portion of the spike and female flowers on the lower part. Later in the season, after the female flowers have been pollinated, male flowers drop off leaving only the female spike to develop.

113

Turk's Cap Lily
Lilium superbum

Liliaceae (Lily) Family

Turk's Cap Lilies inhabit the eastern part of the region covered by this book. Michigan Lilies are native to the westerly areas. Both species are quite similar.

Michigan Lilies are frequently called Turk's Cap, but they are not the same. Turk's Cap is the "star" of the show, displaying a green star in the markings of its throat. Turk's Cap also reaches superb heights, often as tall as 8 feet.

The trio of Michigan Lilies below exhibit spotted orange throat color without a green star. These equally splendid lilies may reach 5 feet in height.

Michigan Lily
Lilium michiganense

Daisy or Common Fleabane
Erigeron philadelphicus
Asteraceae (Aster) Family

Erigeron species, called Fleabanes, are aster-like plants usually blooming earlier than Asters. Ray flowers are more numerous in Fleabanes. **E. philadelphicus** may have over 100 pink rays. Central disk flowers are yellow. Compare Lesser Daisy Fleabane, **E. strigosus**, on next page.

Blue-eyed Grass
Sisyrinchium montanum
Iridaceae (Iris) Family

Names can be misleading. This grassy-leaved plant has *yellow eyes!* Small blue flowers are made up of sepals and petals that look alike (tepals). Each tepal has a distinctive bristle-like tip.

It thrives in grassy meadows, making it hard to find when not in blossom.

115

Lesser Daisy Fleabane
Erigeron strigosus
Asteraceae (Aster) Family

Erigeron species, called Fleabanes, are aster-like plants that usually bloom earlier than Asters. Ray flowers are more numerous in Fleabanes. *E. strigosus* has 50 to 100 rays which are white. Central disk flowers are yellow. Compare *E. philadelphicus*, page 115.

Prairie Sage
Artemisia ludoviciana
Asteraceae (Aster) Family

Primarily a Western species, but has moved eastward into dryer, sunny locations of the Great Lakes region. Leaves are gray from being covered with fine hairs. A sage fragrance is emitted when the plant is crushed. Grows to 2 feet tall. Other ***Artemesia*** species are on pages 186 and 187.

Rabbit's Foot Clover
Trifolium arvense
Fabaceae; Pea or
Legume Family

Rabbit's Foot Clover lines miles of roadsides in some regions. Its soft, silky, pinkish-gray heads appear on low 4 to 12 inch plants. A **European immigrant**, it is an annual, reseeding itself each year.

Northern Hound's Tongue
Cynoglossum boreale
Boraginaceae (**Borage**) **Family**

Arching inflorescences produce 4 bristly nutlets, a trait of Hound's Tongue species. Northern Hound's Tongue has small blue flowers.

Basal leaves are broad (once thought to look like a hound's tongue). Leaves diminish in size as they progress up the stem.

Marsh Hedge Nettle or Marsh Woundwort
Stachys palustris
Lamiaceae (Mint) Family

A tall plant growing up to 3 feet, Marsh Hedge Nettle displays whorls of 6 magenta flowers at intervals along the upper part of the stem. Fine hairs cover all parts of the plant. Here, growing in a wet place, the stem has a deeper red color than the same species found growing in dryer locations.

Northern Bog Orchid
Platanthera hyperborea
Orchidaceae (Orchid) Family

Northern Bog Orchid, aka Northern Green Orchid, ***Habenaria hyperborea***, is adapted to a wide range of environments, from wet to dry, sun to shade, and forest soils to bogs. This temperate climate, terrestrial orchid, stands about 3 feet tall.

Grass Pink
Calopogon pulchellus
Orchidaceae (Orchid) Family

Each plant has only one long, grass-like leaf coming from the base of the stem. Each stem supports 2 or more magenta to pink flowers. The flower is positioned to make it appear upside down with the yellow crested lip at the top or side.

Lightly shaded Sphagnum bogs and swampy areas are places to look for Grass Pinks and Rose Pogonia

Bog Orchids in the Garden
Several bog Orchids are available from specialized suppliers listed on page 301. They are quite easy to grow in an artificial bog.

Joshua Horky

Rose Pogonia
Pogonia ophioglossoides
Orchidaceae (Orchid)Family

Common Sow Thistle
Sonchus oleraceus
Asteraceae (Aster) Family

Sow Thistles are widespread along roadsides, fields and waste places. These tall plants have stems flowing with a white milky juice which is exuded when the stem is broken.

Recurved leaf shape and spines of *S. asper* distinguish it from *S. oleraceus*. **Both of these thistles are introduced species** that have spread to every state and throughout Canada.

Bright yellow, Dandelion-like flowers of both species are attention getters when in bloom.

Spiny-leaved Sow Thistle
Sonchus asper
Asteraceae (Aster) Family

Wild Parsnip
Pastinaca sativa
Apiaceae (Parsley) Family

Wild Parsnip has yellow-green flowers compared to several similar umbel-producing species with white flowers. Its sturdy stems grow 2 to 5 feet tall. Compound leaves have 5 to 15 sessile, toothed leaflets. Being a biennial, it produces a storage taproot during the first year of growth and in the second, it flowers.

Curled Dock
Rumex crispus
Polygonaceae (Buckwheat) Family

Curled Dock has wavy leaf margins. It grows 4 to 6 feet tall. Large branched inflorescences have whorls of small green flowers. Small 3-winged, dry fruits are rusty brown when mature.

Both plants on this page are non-native.

Large-leaved Avens
Geum macrophyllum
Rosaceae (Rose) Family

Growing in wet meadows these plants have inflorescences on open branching stems 1 to 3 feet tall. Flowers that resemble Cinquefoils mature into round, bristly, dry fruits.

Walter Siegmund

Fireweed or Great Willow Herb
Epilobium angustifolium
Onagraceae (Evening Primrose) Family

Striking magenta flowers, in a long inflorescence, bloom steadily in the summer. Red seed capsules form and persist, giving the plant a glow of color in the fall. Later, the capsules break open, releasing a myriad of seeds. Each seed has a tuft of fine hairs, allowing it to be carried away by the wind.

Some references list Fireweed as ***Chamaenerion angustifolium***.

Black or Brown-eyed Susan
Rudbeckia hirta
Asteraceae (Aster) Family

Scentless Chamomile
Tripleurospermum maritimum
Asteraceae (Aster) Family

Black-eyed Susan is a familiar plant seen along roadsides, dry fields and open woods, known by large, yellow flower heads with dark brown centers. Leaves are very hairy as are the stems which grow 1 to 3 feet tall.

Thread-like leaves, flower heads up to 1 1/2 inches wide and lack of fragrance identify this as Scentless Chamomile. Wild Chamomile, *M. chamomilla* (not shown), has smaller flowers and pineapple scent when the leaves are crushed.

Rough Fruited or Sulphur Cinquefoil
Potentilla recta
Rosaceae (Rose) Family

Palmately compound leaves with 5 to 7 long, narrow leaflets is a trait of Sulphur Cinquefoil. Flowers are larger than most Cinquefoils, up to 1 inch in diameter. Stems are up to 2 feet tall.

With its showy yellow flowers, this attractive plant is used in garden landscapes. However it is an **introduced species.**

Crown Vetch
Coronilla varia
Fabaceae (Pea or Legume) Family

Round heads of pink and white flowers are the trademarks of Crown Vetch. Its long, compound leaves divide into many small leaflets. Rambling stems spread over large areas. This is often a plant of choice for erosion control on roadsides and ditch banks. Massive displays of pink are a showy, bloom-time by-product for travelers to enjoy. It is an **introduced species.**

Pipsissewa
Chimaphila umbellata
Ericaceae (Heath) Family

Pipsissewa inhabits Jack and Red Pine forests. These unique plants have whorls of dark green, leathery leaves.

Nodding, waxy, pink and white flowers hang on top of a slender stem. These beautiful flowers give way to formation of brown capsules containing seeds.

Wintergreen
Gaultheria procumbens
Ericaceae (Heath) Family

Leaves of Wintergreen persist over winter, becoming red-bronze in color. Red berries produced the previous summer remain all winter if not eaten by critters.

By mid-summer, the bronze leaves have been replaced by bright green leaves. White bell-shaped flowers dangle under the new leaves. In time new berries will be produced and the cycle continues.

In the Garden
Easy to naturalize under pines mixed with other pine forest perennials or as a mass planting for a ground cover.

Swamp Smartweed
Persicaria coccineum
Polygonaceae
(Buckwheat) Family

Like Water Smartweed (page 157), Swamp Smartweed has an aquatic and terrestrial form as shown here. In this terrestrial habitat, Swamp Smartweed has an erect form. Inflorescences are longer in ***P. coccineum*** than in ***P. amphibium***.

Arrow-Leaved
Tearthumb
Persicaria sagittata
Polygonaceae
(Buckwheat) Family

Tearthumb grows in wet places. It has weak stems which have small spines. Sometimes called "Scratch-grass".

Tower Mustard
Arabis glabra
Brassicaceae (Mustard) Family

Tower Mustard has a basal rosette of slightly lobed, lance-shaped leaves. Upper leaves have lobes that clasp the stem. Purplish coloration of stem and leaves is common.

Flowers vary from white to a yellow color. Long thin seed pods point upward and are held close to the stem. Plants may grow to 4 feet tall.

Siliques (Seed Pods)

133

Canada Lettuce
Lactuca canadensis
Asteraceae (Aster) Family

Yellow flower heads, like miniature Dandelions, cover the top of Canada Lettuce plants which grow 3 to 6 feet tall. Leaves are variable, some being deeply lobed and others only slightly lobed, if at all.

Like Dandelions, these seeds are tufted and blow away with the wind. The reddish-purple stem of the plant in the photo is not necessarily typical, but may be colored due to growing conditions.

Marsh or Bedstraw Bellflower
Campanula aparinoides
Campanulaceae (Bluebell) Family

Flowers, white or tinged with pale blue, grace weak stems that resemble bedstraw. Using Sensitive Fern as support, these stems are able to hang on with tiny, grasping bristles.

Marsh Bellflower grows in wet, sunny meadows or bogs.

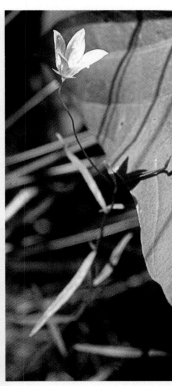

135

Common Mullein (right)
Verbascum thapsus
Scrophulariaceae (**Snapdragon**) **Family**

Mullein towers above other plants, growing to a height of 6 to 8 feet. Large velvety leaves (up to 12 inches long) and a thick, woolly stem give this plant a character all its own. Being a biennial, in its first year of growth a large rosette of basal leaves form. In the second year, the tall flower stalk is produced.

Wormseed Mustard
Erysimum cheiranthoides
Brassicaceae (**Mustard**) **Family**

Wormseed Mustard grows up to 3 feet tall. Leaves are long and narrow with just a few "teeth" along the edges. Long, thin seed pods, once formed, are held erect and somewhat parallel to the stem.

Bristly Sarsaparilla
Aralia hispida
Araliaceae (Ginseng) Family

Flower stalks branch from bristly, above-ground stems, a trait that sets this species apart from Wild Sarsaparilla on page 26. Round umbels of white flowers produce a display of blue-black berries. Bristly Sarsaparilla grows to nearly 4 feet tall in peat land and open woods.

137

Marsh or Common Skullcap
Scutellaria galericulata var. *epilobiifolia*
Lamiaceae (Mint) Family

Marsh Skullcap typically has one flower in each leaf axil. With opposite leaves and flowers in each leaf axil pointing the same direction, the flowers appear to be "twins" arising from the same node.

As the name indicates, wet places like marshes, lake shores, and swampy meadows are places to look for this plant. It grows 1 to 3 feet tall.

Downy Rattlesnake Plantain
Goodyera pubescens
Orchidaceae (Orchid) Family

The distinct netted pattern of the leaves and white midrib band are standard clues to identification of **G. pubescens.** Deciduous forests with acidic soil is its preferred habitat.

Yellow Fringed Orchid
Platanthera ciliaris
Orchidaceae (Orchid) Family

Yellow Fringed Orchid is seldom seen. Its range is in the Eastern part of the Great Lakes region. Very rare today, it is listed as endangered in several states. On the positive side, research is being conducted in order to propagate and to reintroduce this lovely Orchid back into the wild.

Purple Fringed Orchid
Platanthera psycodes
Orchidaceae (Orchid) Family

Growing in diverse habitats, Purple Fringed Orchid may be found in shade or full sunlight, in organic or mineral soils, in wet woods or in meadows.

Its stem grows up to 3 feet high including the inflorescence.

Purple Fringed Orchid's scientific name is also listed as **Habenaria psycodes** in many references.

Water Plantain
Alisma triviale
Alismataceae
(Arrowhead) Family

White, 3-petaled flowers of Water Plantain are usually borne in whorls of 4. Branched flower stalks arise from a circular base of upright, elliptical leaves. These plants typically grow in shallow water, muddy ditches, or edges of ponds.

A similar species *A. subcordatum*, Small Water Plantain (not shown), has smaller flowers with petals no longer in length than the green sepals.

141

Deptford Pink
Dianthus armeria
Caryophyllaceae (**Pink**) **Family**

Pink petals dotted with white and having "teeth" on the edges are clues for recognizing Deptford Pink. Long narrow leaves grow on a slender stem, 12 to 18 inches tall. Its grassy habitat makes it a natural along roadsides, meadows, and clearings in woods.

Notches at the petal tips are a trait of the Pink Family. Some petals look like they have been trimmed with pinking shears, and so are called "pinks." Pinks come in a variety of colors.

Deptford Pink is an **introduced species.**

Yellow Water Lily
Nuphar lutea
Nymphaeaceae (Water Lily) Family

A plant of many names, Yellow Water Lily is known as Bullhead Lily, Spatterdock, Pond Lily, and Cow Lily. By whatever name, it is common to many lakes, quiet streams and ponds throughout the region.

Large floating leaves up to 12 inches long grow from a submerged rhizome.

Flowers have a whorl of 5 or 6 yellow or yellow-green sepals that resemble fleshy petals. Many small petals that look like stamens are inside the large, cup-shaped sepals. The center of the flower has a stigma that looks like a "toadstool." This unusual flower is held above the water on its own thick stalk.

Fragrant Water Lily
Nymphaea odorata
Nymphaeaceae (**Water Lily**) **Family**

Fragrant Water Lily, also called Sweet Scented Water Lily, displays showy white petals. Round floating leaves are usually purplish underneath.

A similar lily, White or Tuberous Water Lily (***N. tuberosa***) does not have fragrance, and its leaves are green on the underside.

Swamp Milkweed
Asclepias incarnata
Apocynaceae
(Dogbane) Family

Name Change

The genus *Asclepias* was in *Asclepadaceae* or Milkweed Family.

A recent taxonomic change has it placed in *Apocynaceae*, but the former Milkweed Family is given a sub-family name: *Asclepiadoideae*.

Standing as much as 3 to 4 feet tall in wet marshes or lake shores, Swamp Milkweed blooms with a striking cluster of rose-purple flowers. Unique milkweed flower structure is evident, shown by downward-pointing petals in the photo below.

Above the petals are 5 erect hoods, each having a curved crest pointing inward. At the flower's center is a white stigma.

In the Garden

Although at home in wet places, swamp milkweed will perform quite well in dryer conditions. It makes a nice addition to an upland wildflower garden for a tall plant with bright flowers in the background.

Being a Milkweed, it also attracts the Monarch Butterfly.

145

Purple Loosestrife
Lythrum salicaria
Lythraceae
(Loosestrife) Family

Purple Loosestrife, **a non-native plant**, has a dense spike of purple to pink flowers on 2 to 4 foot stems. **A handsome plant, once considered choice for home gardens, is now listed as a noxious weed.**

When established in swamps and marshes, it grows rampantly, crowding out native plants.

Rough Bedstraw
Galium asprellum
Rubiaceae (Bedstraw) Family

Stems of Rough Bedstraw are square, weak and somewhat prickly (rough to the touch). Leaves less than 1 inch long are usually in whorls of 6, but sometimes there are 4 or 5 in a whorl.

Small white flowers are abundant.

Cleavers, *G. aparine* (not pictured), is similar in appearance except it has bigger leaves 1 to 3 inches long.

Blue Vervain
Verbena hastata
Verbenaceae (**Vervain**) **Family**

Blue Vervain flower clusters are slender spikes having only a few lavender-blue flowers open at one time.

Stems grow 2 to 5 feet tall with opposite, coarsely-toothed leaves. Lower leaves are sometimes lobed.

It grows in dry, open habitats.

In the Garden
Blue Vervain works well in a wildflower garden. It gives a unique character to a sunny open spot in late summer.

Fringed Loosestrife
Lysimachia ciliata
Myrsinaceae (Myrsine) Family

Formerly listed in *Primulaceae*

The "fringes" of Fringed Loosestrife are on the upper edge of leaf petioles. Indicated by the yellow circle.

Nodding yellow flowers have contrasting bright red-orange eyes and tiny "teeth" at the tips of the petals.

Plants grow 1 to 3 feet tall in a range of moist habitats.

Orange-fruited
Horse Gentian
Triosteum aurantiacum
Caprifoliaceae
(Honeysuckle) Family

Ilona Loser

Orange fruits circle each node, having developed from the dull-red, stalkless flowers.

A similar plant, Wild Coffee, ***T. perfoliantum*** (not shown), has leaves that are joined at the base surrounding the stem. Orange-fruited Horse Gentian leaves are sessile to the stem.

In the Garden
Fringed Loosestrife is often used as a landscape plant. It does tend to be invasive, but controllable.

149

Swamp Candles
Lysimachia terrestris
Myrsinaceae (Myrsine) Family

Shaded by a tree on a lake shore, Swamp Candles is in a typical habitat. These plants, with terminal flower clusters, grow about 2 feet tall.

Marsh Cinquefoil
Comarum palustre
Rosaceae (Rose) Family

Name Change
Formerly listed as
Potentilla palustris

Marsh Cinquefoil has large red sepals longer than smaller red petals. Together the petals and sepals form flowers about one inch in diameter.

Stems up to 2 feet long tend to be sprawling in their wet bog or swamp habitats.

151

Woolly Yarrow
Achillea lanulosa
Asteraceae (**Aster**) **Family**

Woolly Yarrow stems and leaves are densely covered with matted pubescense making them look dark gray.

A. lanulosa is native to the western part of the Great Lakes region. A similar species, Common Yarrow ***Achillea millefolium*** (of **European origin**), has also naturalized throughout the region.

Both species have finely divided leaves often described as fern-like, but Common Yarrow is not woolly.

Common Agrimony or Tall Hairy Agrimony
Agrimonia gryposepala
Rosaceae (Rose) Family

From a distance, Agrimony inflorescences can be mistaken for Yellow Sweet Clover (page 110), but their flowers are definitely different. A closer look reveals tiny 5-petaled, radial, yellow flowers typical of the Rose Family.

Leaves of Agrimony are compound with several leaflets.

Fruits have hooked prickles which stick tightly to clothing and animal fur.

Evening Primrose
Oenothera biennis
Onagraceae
(Evening Primrose) Family

These flowers will open wide in the evening, revealing 4 large petals, each up to one inch long. Evening Primrose may grow up to 6 feet high. Although native, it tends to become weedy in a garden situation.

Common St. John's Wort
Hypericum perforatum
Clusiaceae
(St. John's Wort) Family

Dark dots on otherwise clear yellow petals and conspicuous stamens are natural characteristics of St. John's Wort.

Narrow, oblong, oppositely arranged, sessile leaves are attached to the main stems and branches.

This *Clusiaceae*, **a European introduction**, is a common weed along roadsides and open fields, growing more that 2 feet tall.

Round-leaved Sundew
Drosera rotundifolia
Droseraceae (Sundew) Family

One Bloom at a Time

Sundew plants are carnivorous. In the nutrient-poor Sphagnum bog, Sundew leaves are adapted for catching insects. Trapped insects, a good nitrogen source, are digested and their nutrients are absorbed into the plant's system.

Spoon-shaped leaves, attractively colored, have many glandular hairs that secrete sweet droplets at their tips as "bait" for the insects.

Nodding Flower Stalk

Leaves with hairs to catch insects

Early Goldenrod
Solidago juncea
Asteraceae (**Aster**) **Family**

Early Goldenrod is described as plume-like. Basal leaves are broad and toothed, but leaves on the upper part of the stem are narrow and entire.

Goldenrod Trivia

Blooms of Goldenrods seem to mark the transition to late summer. Various species come into bloom throughout the remainder of the growing season.

Due to many of the species being so similar they are difficult to identify, flower head "forms" characterize general groups of Goldenrods. These forms include plume-like, elm-branched, club-like, wand-like and flat-topped.

More trivia on page 193.

Water Smartweed
Persicaria amphibia

Water Smartweed is similar to Swamp Smartweed (page 132). Both have aquatic and terrestrial forms. Here the aquatic form of ***P. amphibium*** is growing in typical habitat. Note the flower stalks are held above the water with a pink cluster of flowers being about 1 1/2 inches long.

Floating leaves of Water Smartweed are broader and more blunt on the tip than the terrestrial form.

A Name Change

Smartweeds have traditionally been in ***Polygonatum*** Genus. More recently, they have been assigned to ***Persicaria***.

They continue to be in ***Polygonaceae*** or the **Buckwheat Family**.

Shinleaf
Pyrola elliptica
Ericaceae (Heath) Family

Blooming later than other **Pyrola** species (page 93), Shinleaf grows through the mulch of pine forests.

Leaves of Shinleaf are large, egg-shaped and not as thick or leathery as other **Pyrola**.

White flowers bloom on slender 6 to 10 inch stalks.

Common Speedwell
Veronica officinalis
Plantaginaceae (Plantain) Family

Common Speedwell has hairy, trailing stems with finely-toothed, egg-shaped leaves. Dainty lavender flowers have 4 petals. A trait of **Veronica** shows 3 similar sized petals and one, the lower petal, being decidedly smaller.

A non-native **from Eurasia**.

Northern Willow Herb
Epilobium ciliatum
ssp.glandulosum
Onagraceae
(Evening Primrose)Family

Small, four-petaled pink flowers are deeply notched at the tip of each petal. Notched petal tips are displayed by many species, but it is a specific trait of the Pink Family. Pink Family flowers usually have 5 petals.

Plants grow 1 to 3 feet tall and have shiny green leaves that are edged with shallow teeth.

Seeds with whitish hairs are produced in long, brown seed pods.

Clustered Bellflower
Campanula glomerata
Campanulaceae
(Bluebell) Family

Selections of Clustered Bellflower are extensively used in home landscapes. It is an **alien that has escaped** into natural areas and along roadsides. Plants grow 1 to 2 feet tall and produce an attractive tight cluster of blue flowers at the tip of the stem.

Wild Mint
Mentha arvensis
Lamiaceae (Mint) Family

Wild Mint has lavender (and occasionally white) flowers tightly clustered in its leaf axils. Leaves are oblong, serrated and have a strong mint smell when crushed. Hairy stems grow 1 to 2 feet tall, usually in moist open places, but sometimes in dry locations.

161

Joe Pye Weed
Eupatorium maculatum
Asteraceae (Aster) Family

Spotted Joe Pye Weed is another name given this plant because its stem may be purple-spotted rather than solid purple.

Toothed leaves are in whorls of 4 or 5 on a stem 3 to 5 feet tall.

As flower buds open, the inflorescence becomes more flattened on top and is covered with small, fuzzy-looking pink flowers.

Joe Pye Weed in the Garden

A native plant, Joe Pye Weed has made its way into home gardens and landscapes where tall plants are desired. It is easy to grow and readily available.

It is really not "weedy" as the name implies!

Common or Broadleaf Arrowhead
Sagittaria latifolia
Alismataceae (Arrowhead) Family

Leaves of Common Arrowhead are arrow-shaped and can have very narrow to broad lobes. Flowers are in whorls of 3 and each flower has 3 white petals. Quiet, shallow water of ponds, lake shores, and slow-moving streams provide habitat.

Arrowhead in the Garden

Broadleaf Arrowhead gives a unique texture and form to a water or bog garden.

163

Queen Anne's Lace
Daucus carota
Apiaceae (**Parsley**) **Family**

Queen Anne's Lace is Wild Carrot. A rosette of finely divided leaves and a fleshy root similar to the roots and leaves of garden variety carrots marks the first year of growth. In the second year, a long stem up to 3 or 4 feet is topped with a flat umbel of tiny white flowers.

Stiff, forked bracts under the umbel separate this plant from other white flowered, umbel-producing species.

It is **native to Europe** and was brought over as a medicinal plant. Unfortunately it has become naturalized and become a weed in many places.

Hoary Alyssum
Berteroa incana
Brassicaceae
(**Mustard**) **Family**

Hoary Alyssum grows about 1 to 2 feet tall. Lance-shaped leaves are grayish due to a downy covering.

Flowers have 4 deeply cleft petals thickly clustered on a flower stalk that continues to elongate. The result is a long stalk with flattened oval seed capsules along its side.

Hoary Alyssum is an **introduced species** that has become a noxious weed throughout the region.

Pearly Everlasting
Anaphalis margaritacea
Asteraceae (Aster) Family

Flowers of Pearly Everlasting are in rounded heads that have many dry, white, petal-like bracts surrounding yellow disk flowers. Male and female flowers are produced on separate plants.

Stems growing 1 to 3 feet tall are woolly and have long narrow leaves which are also woolly on the underside.

Dry, open places are preferred habitat, but Pearly Everlasting also grows in light-shaded forest edges.

In the Garden
Pearly Everlasting is an attractive addition to an open, sunny area. It has a tendency to spread, but is usually easy to control.

Butter-and-Eggs
Linaria vulgaris
Plantaginaceae (**Plantain**) **Family**

Formerly in *Scrophulariaceae* (**Snapdragon**) **Family**

Bi-colored yellow and orange flowers grow on a spike-like stalk up to 3 feet tall.

Gardeners, delighted with their pretty Snapdragon-like blossoms, brought them to America **from Europe**.

Beauty is only blossom deep, for it spreads rapidly in a garden and on to any dry, sunny location where soil has been disturbed.

Unfortunately, Butter and Eggs is a persistant weed.

Tall or Giant Sunflower
Helianthus giganteus
Asteraceae (Aster) Family

Tall Sunflower is a perennial that thrives in wet places. Its alternate, lance-shaped leaves are rough with little or no stalk attaching them to the reddish-colored, 4 to 10 foot stem.

Among the many sunflower species in this region, all have similar characteristics. Commercially grown sunflowers have been developed by selecting and breeding desirable traits, especially those of **H. annuus**, one of the wild sunflowers.

167

Jewelweed or
Spotted Touch-me-not
Impatiens capensis
Balsaminaceae (Touch-me-not) Family

This annual plant is closely related to the popular tropical **Impatiens** raised extensively as bedding plants in shady landscapes. A native of the temperate climate, Jewelweed thrives in wet, shady places.

Jewelweed stems, about 2 to 5 feet tall, are hollow and succulent, but support orange spotted yellow flowers as they dangle from long stalks.

Seed capsules, about 1 inch long, become plump when ripe and "explode" on contact with anything that touches them. The force twists the capsule inside out. Note the immature capsule (below) and spent capsule being held by the photographer.

Pickerel Weed
Pontederia cordata
Pontederiaceae (Water Hyacinth) Family

Each large pickerelweed plant produces 1 spike of small flowers. It is usually about 3 feet tall, with long, heart-shaped leaves.

A flower spike rises above the leaves with 1 leaf growing behind it. Deep blue flowers bloom in succession from the bottom up to the top of the spike.

There may be 2 feet or more of stem submerged with leaves and flowers above water.

This habitat of shallow, quiet water. is also conducive to the pickerel fish, hence it's name.

169

Harebell
Campanula rotundifolia
Campanulaceae (Bluebell) Family

Harebell seems to grow in some of the most inhospitable places imaginable, such as this rocky ledge along Lake Superior's north shore. Thin wiry stems, rarely over 15 inches tall, have fine leaves and delicate, bell-shaped flowers.

Harebell in the Garden
Commonly used in landscaping, Harebell is most effective in naturalistic situations as depicted by the photos.

Creeping Bellflower
Campanula rapunculoides
Campanulaceae (Bluebell) Family

Creeping Bellflower, also called **European Bellflower**, is a robust plant growing to 1 to 3 feet tall. It forms large patches on roadsides and open areas, propagating by spreading rootstocks as well as by seed dispersal.

Nodding, blue, bell-shaped flowers over 1 inch in length develop on just one side of the flower stalk.

WARNING: It has pretty flowers, but it spreads quickly and takes over in a garden. **Extremely hard to eradicate**. There are plenty of gentle Bellflowers to cultivate without introducing this one!

Canada Thistle
Cirsium arvense
Asteraceae (Aster) **Family**

Flowers of Canada Thistle are pretty, but oh, those prickly leaves!

Surely our **European or Asian** ancestors didn't bring this one to North America on purpose.

Underground stems (rhizomes) provide the invading process of this plant, making it hard to eradicate once established. Grows 1 to 3 feet tall.

At least one redeeming fact is that many butter-flies are attracted to the flowers and feed on them.

Bull Thistle
Cirsium vulgare
Asteraceae (Aster) Family

A giant among thistles, Bull Thistle lives up to its name: One doesn't toy with this plant. Armed with sharp, prickly leaves and stems, Bull Thistle needs careful handling. A single plant can grow up to 6 feet tall and 3 feet wide. This **imported plant** has become established in every state in the U. S. and every Province in Canada.

Enchanter's Nightshade
Circaea quadrisulcata
Onagraceae
(Evening Primrose) Family

Innocent-looking, delicate white flowers, clearly notched at the tip of each petal, bloom in loose clusters. The flowers seem inviting, but with time, pear-shaped fruits covered with hooked bristles develop. These tiny bristles cling tightly to clothing and fur, making the fruits difficult to remove.

Leaves are opposite and elliptical. Lower leaves have long petioles, but those higher on the stem are nearly sessile.

Turtlehead
Chelone glabra
Plantaginaceae (Plantain) Family

Formerly in Scrophulariaceae (Snapdragon) Family

Turtlehead thrives in damp places, growing up to 3 feet tall. Flowers of **C. glabra** are about 1 inch long and have an arched upper lip that resembles a turtle's head. Leaves are opposite, lance-shaped and have fine serrations.

Turtlehead in the Garden
Other Turtlehead species **C. lyoni** (pink) and **C. obliqua** (red), are not as prevalent in this region, but are chosen along with **C. glabra** as landscape plants for their lovely fall bloom.

Common Tansy
Tanacetum vulgare
Asteraceae (Aster) Family

Tansy, an **introduced species**, once favored as a garden flower, has become a weed, spreading over roadsides, vacant lots, open fields and waste places. It forms large patches.

Finely divided leaves release fragrance when crushed. Button-like, yellow flower heads form flat- topped inflorescences.

Daylily
Hemerocallis fulva
Hemerocallidaceae
(Daylily) Family

Previously in
Lilliaceae (Lily) Family

Daylily flowers are without spots as compared to other wild lilies of the region (page 114).

Long grass-like leaves form clumps. Leaves and flower stalks of Daylily arise from the crown of the plant at ground level. In the photo center left, Daylily foliage makes a good backdrop for the Geranium in bloom. Soon the Daylily will come into its own bloom-time.

Originally **from Japan**, *H. fulva* was brought to North America as a horticultural garden plant. It is now widely naturalized.

Hemerocallis species have pleased gardeners for generations. Today there are hundreds of beautiful cultivars that have been produced and are commercially available.

Tiger Lily
Lilium lancifolium
Liliaceae (Lily) Family

Like Turk's Cap and Michigan Lilies on page 114, Tiger Lily has orange, nodding, spotted flowers. However, *L. lancifolium* can be distinguished by purple stems, alternately arranged leaves, and little bulblets in the leaf axils on the upper part of the stem.

Tiger Lily is a **native of Eastern Asia**.

Public domain

177

Nipplewort
Lapsana communis
Asteraceae (Aster) Family

Petite flower heads of a soft yellow color are only half an inch across and bloom on stiff, slender, branched stems. Stems grow up to 3 feet tall. Egg-shaped leaves are slightly toothed and may be lobed on the lower portion of the stem.

A naturalized species **from Europe**.

Common Burdock
Arctium minus
Asteraceae (Aster) Family

Attractive pink but bristly flower heads of Burdock ripen into clinging burs.

Oval leaves are alternately arranged on a thick, grooved and hollow stem growing up to 5 feet tall.

Only a basal rosette of leaves forms the first season, but this clump may be up to 3 feet in diameter. Like a true biennial, the second season's growth produces the flower stalk. A natualized species **from Europe**.

Hemp Nettle
Galeopsis tetrahit
Lamiaceae (**Mint**) **Family**

Hemp Nettle has two-lipped flowers, the upper lip projecting over the opening and the 3 lobed lower lip having two prominent "nipples" projecting upward at its base. Flowers are up to three-fourths inch long.

Bristly stems bear oval, coarsely-toothed leaves that resemble those of Stinging Nettle (page 204), but there are no stinging hairs on Hemp Nettle leaves.

White Vervain
Verbena urticifolia
Verbenaceae (**Vervain**) **Family**

Diminutive white flowers appearing on slender spikes identifies White Vervain. Leaves are opposite and coarsely serrated. White Vervain grows 3 to 5 feet tall on stems that are usually hairy.

White Lettuce
Prenanthes alba
Asteraceae (Aster) Family

White Lettuce is one of a group of plants called Rattlesnake Root. Others include Tall Rattlesnake Root **(P. trifoliata)**, Lion's Foot **(P. serpentaria)** and Boott's Rattlesnake Root **(P. boottii)**. All of these species have leaves that vary widely in structure, a curious growth habit.

In White Lettuce, leaves vary from triangular shape on the plant pictured on the facing page to the deeply lobed leaves shown right. Stems are usually purple growing 2 to 5 feet tall.

Flowers of White Lettuce are identified with the brownish colored hairs beneath the sepals called the pappus. Flower color may range from white to pinkish.

White Lettuce Flowers
(pink form)

**White Lettuce
Flowers**

**Brownish Pappus
Under Sepals**

**White Lettuce with Triangular
Leaves**

Musk Mallow
Malva moschata
Malvaceae (Mallow) Family

Indentations at the petal tips identify this as Musk Mallow along with leaves divided into narrow segments. Flowers may be white as well as pink with many stamens fused to a central pistil, a characteristic of the Mallow Family.

These plants, escaped from cultivation, amay be found along roadsides and waste places.

Horseweed
Conyza canadensis
Asteraceae (Aster) Family

Flowers of Horseweed are in tiny heads about one-eighth inch long. These heads remain tightly closed until small tufted seeds form and are released to be scattered by the wind. Narrow, lance-shaped leaves are on hairy stems. Plants may be as much as 7 feet tall.

185

Tall Wormwood
Artemisia campestris
ssp. caudata
Asteraceae (Aster) Family

Wormwood and Mugwort are names applied to several ***Artemisia*** species, creating certain confusion about plant identity. Dry, sandy areas, including beaches and dunes of the Great Lakes, are likely habitats.

Tall Wormwood, ***A. caudata***, has very finely divided and forked, silvery-colored leaves. Numerous, small, nodding flower heads line up on long stalks. Red stems to 2 feet tall are characteristic of this ***Artemisia***. Prairie Sage on page 117 is another ***Artemisia***.

This species is native.

Absinthe Wormwood
Artemisia absinthium
Asteraceae (Aster) Family

Gray-green, drooping flower heads of Absinthe Wormwood are larger than those of Tall Wormwood. Leaves are deeply cut on the lower part of the stem, becoming progressively smaller on the upper portion of the plant. **Native to Eurasia and Northern Africa**.

Wild Bergamot
Monarda fistulosa
Lamiaceae (Mint) Family

Dense rounded heads of pinkish to pale lavender flowers top square, erect stems 2 to 3 feet tall. Bees commonly visit these flowers for the nectar used in honey production.

Other species of Bergamot in the region include Bee Balm or Oswego Tea *(M. didyma)* and Purple Bergamot *(M. media)* (not pictured).

Wild Bergamont In the Garden

Besides being an attractive perennial, this Colorful plant attracts both butterflies and hummingbirds.

Several cultivars have been introduced for landscape use.

Gray Headed Coneflower
Ratibida pinnata
Asteraceae (Aster) Family

Long yellow ray flowers droop downward in **R. pinnata**, and the central disk (seed producing) flowers are on a long "cone."

Leaves are deeply cut into 3 to 7 narrow, toothed segments. A hairy stem grows 3 to 5 feet tall.

Dry meadows and roadsides are natural habitats for Gray Headed Coneflower.

Coneflower in the Garden
Makes a nice landscape plant in a sunny prairie-like location.

Gray Goldenrod
Solidago nemoralis
Asteraceae (**Aster**) **Family**

Gray Goldenrod has "plume-like" inflorescences. Short stems, 10 to 24 inches. Narrow leaves are fuzzy, giving them a gray-green color. Tiny leaflets grow out of the leaf axils.

Showy Goldenrod
Solidago speciosa
Asteraceae (Aster) Family

Flower clusters point upward in Showy Goldenrod, a "club-like" type. Flowers on the lower part of the stem develop later than terminal ones. The inflorescence widens at the bottom.

Greater or Late Goldenrod
Solidago gigantea
Asteraceae (Aster) Family

Goldenrod's gentle giant, **S. gigantea**, grows up to 7 feet tall topped with a large plume-like inflorescence.

Stems may be green or purplish. Leaves are sharply toothed and lance-shaped. Greater Goldenrod thrives in both moist and dry places.

Prairie or Missouri Goldenrod
Solidago missouriensis
Asteraceae (Aster) Family

Open, drooping branches of flower heads identify "elm-branched" types of Goldenrod. Clues to Prairie Goldenrod are smooth, lance-shaped leaves, mostly with 3 "nerves" (major veins); lower leaves may have serrations. Stems are smooth and hairless and grow up to 3 feet tall.

More Goldenrod Trivia

Goldenrod pollen has been berated as the culprit for causing hay fever. Goldenrods are insect pollinated. This pollen does not readily become wind borne. However the real culprit is another Aster Family plant, Common Ragweed (page 201). Its pollen is wind blown and does cause allergic reactions.

Galls often form on Goldenrod stems (below). Insect larvae grow inside the stem, forming the enlargement. ***S. gigantea*** (opposite page) and ***S. canadensis*** (page 210) are prone to this kind of invasion.

Taxonomists have identified over 60 species of Goldenrod in Northeast United States and adjacent Canada. Numerous species are hard to identify: Minute characteristics must be used to classify them. To complicate the identities even more, hybridization between species may occur.

Insect larvae Galls

Lance or Grass-leaved Goldenrod
Euthamia (Solidago) graminifolia*
Asteraceae (Aster) Family

*Many references list this in genus **Solidago**.

Narrow, lance-shaped leaves and a "flat-topped" inflorescence type identify this Goldenrod. It grows 2 to 4 feet tall in moist or dry places.

Flat-topped Aster
Doellingeria umbellata
Asteraceae (Aster) Family

A thick, flat cluster of white flower heads (each with only 7 to 14 ray flowers and yellow disk flowers in the center of each inflorescence) describes Flat-topped Aster.

It has lance-shaped, entire leaves on a stem reaching up to 7 feet high.

Large-leaved Aster
Eurybia macrophylla
Asteraceae (**Aster**) **Family**

Large-leaved Aster is easy to recognize by its huge basal leaves which reach 4 to 8 inches wide. Many deciduous forest floors become covered with this Aster in the spring-time.

Upper leaves are smaller and sessile. Disk flowers are yellow while rays are lavender and number about 10 to 20.

Lowrie's Aster
Symphyotrichum lowrieanum
Asteraceae (Aster) Family

Lowrie's Aster, with a distinctive heart-shaped leaf, has a flat, winged petiole. Purplish stems are common. Flower heads with 8 to 20 lavender rays are arranged in long, open panicles.

Calico, Necklace or Side-flowering Aster
Symphyotrichum lateriflorum
Asteraceae (Aster) Family

White or purple-tinged ray flowers surround a purple disk on **A. *lateriflorus***. These small flower heads tend to be on one side of the flower stalk.

Spotted Knapweed
Centaurea maculosa
Asteraceae (Aster) Family

Spotted Knapweed has gray-colored, deeply-cut leaves and pink to purple thistle-like flowers. Much branched, stiff stems give the plant an "open" appearance. The "spot" of Spotted Knapweed comes from a black tip on the bracts surrounding the flower heads.

This is an invasive weed with **European origin.** It grows along roadsides, in gravel pits and sandy areas. It is also phytotoxic, (poisonous to other plants).

Rattlesnake Master
Eryngium yuccifolium
Apiaceae (Parsley) Family

Most Parsley Family plants have flat-topped umbels, but Rattlesnake Master has a round, tight flower cluster. These flowers are small and white.

Stiff, Yucca-like leaves with spiny edges can grow to 3 feet long. Overall, Rattlesnake Master may reach 4 feet in height.

Common Ragweed
Ambrosia artemisiifolia
Asteraceae (Aster) Family

A slender spike-like inflorescence, 3 to 5 inches long, carries tiny green flowers, the culprits that discharge hay-fever-inducing pollen into the air. Leaves are finely divided into numerous segments. Plants may grow up to 6 feet tall.

Chicory
Cichorium intybus
Asteraceae (Aster) Family

Look for Chicory in the morning. By afternoon, the flowers have closed for the day!

Flower heads with striking blue rays grace Chicory plants and are often found along the roadside.

Each flower ray has a conspicuous serrated tip. Flower heads may reach 1.5 inches in diameter.

Dried roots are roasted and ground to flavor coffee or used as a coffee substitute. Dandelion-like basal leaves can be gathered in the spring when they are tender and used as salad greens.

An introduced plant gone wild.

Bouncing Bet or Soapwort
Saponaria officinalis
Caryophyllaceae (**Pink**) Family

Bouncing Bet may have single or double flowers, either pink or white.

Wort means plant; Soapwort translates "soap plant." The presence of saponin produces soap-like suds.

Pioneers imported it to use as a detergent.

Pale Corydalis
Capnoides sempervirens
Fumariaceae (Bleeding Heart) Family

In close-up or in mass, these pink flowers with yellow tips are handsome. Attractive lobed, pale-green leaves grow on branched stems. Pale Corydalis plants reach 2 feet in height. Slender seed capsules produce many, many tiny black seeds. Compare Yellow Corydalis on page 87.

Stinging Nettle
Urtica dioica
Urticaceae (Nettle) Family

An encounter with Stinging Nettle is one to be avoided! Tiny stinging hairs cover the leaves and stems. Any touch on bare skin could produce a painful dermatitis.

String-like clusters of diminutive greenish flowers hang from the leaf axils. Leaves are heart-shaped and heavily serrated. Plants grow 3 to 5 feet tall.

Purple Giant Hyssop
Agastache scrophulariifolia
Lamiaceae (Mint) Family

Fragrant lavender-purple flowers circle a crowded spike. Coarsely-toothed leaves have a hairy, white underside. Stems are reddish in color and grow 2 to 5 feet tall.

In the Garden
This plant is attractive to bees, birds and butterflies. Easily started from seed which can be acquired from specialty nurseries. A consistently moist soil is ideal. Tolerates full sun, but will also perform in light shade.

Great Blue Cardinal Flower
Lobelia siphilitica
Campanulaceae (Bluebell) Family

Native to essentially all of Eastern US and Canada. Found growing in moist habitats. May grow up to 3 feet tall. Bloom time is late summer.

Hooded Ladies'-tresses
Spiranthes romanzoffiana
Orchidaceae (Orchid) Family

Hooded Ladies'-tresses is a small orchid usually found in open meadows or sphagnum swamps. They may reach 10 to 15 inches in height including the flower spike.

In the Garden

With the characteristics of blue colored flowers and late summer blooming, Great Blue Cardinal Flower is a prime candidate for landscape use. It has a long blooming season as well.

Seeds or started plants are available at specialty nurseries or garden centers. A consistently moist soil is ideal. Tolerates full sun, but will also perform in light shade.

Indian Pipe
Monotropa uniflora
Ericaceae (Heather) Family

Indian Pipe thrives in dense shade of moist woodlands. It doesn't have green chlorophyll, therefore it doesn't need light for photosynthesis. A symbiotic relationship exists with other organisms. Food is absorbed from hosts (other green plants or fungi).

Like Coral Root (page 44), it is a flowering, seed producing plant. The photo illustrates flower buds pointed upward and about to open. Flowers are white. Upon opening, they bend downward to form a "pipe." Scale-like leaves are small and turn brown as the plant ages. White stems grow 4 to 8 inches tall.

Hard-leaved or Stiff Goldenrod
Solidago rigida
Asteraceae (Aster) Family

Located in a "flat top" cluster, flower heads of Stiff Goldenrod are larger than most other Goldenrods. Stems grow up to 5 feet tall and carry broad leaves that are thick, having a cardboard-like texture.

Zig-zag Goldenrod
Solidago flexicaulis
Asteraceae (Aster) Family

Small groups of flower heads alternate from side to side at the base of oval leaves giving this Goldenrod stem a "zig-zag" appearance. Thriving in woodland habitats, plants grow up to 3 feet in height.

Heath or Many Flowered Aster
Symphyotrichum ericoides
Asteraceae (Aster) Family

Heath Asters grow in dry, open fields and meadows. Stems with numerous branches become covered with narrow leaves 0.5 to 1.5 inches long. Stems grow to 3 feet or more. A profuse display of small white flower clusters appear in late summer.

Name Changes
According to Wikipedia, there were nearly 600 species listed in Genus *Aster* in Eurasia and North America. The North American natives have been moved from Genus *Aster* to one of the following Genera:

Eucephalus
Eurybia
Oreostemma
Lonactis
Symphyotrichum.

More about Asters
Asters rival Goldenrod for number of species in the region, with over 60 being identified and described. As a matter of course, Asters commonly hybridize, producing intermediate forms which makes their identification even more confusing. Colors range from white to purple or blue. Many species are useful **"In the Garden"**.

Canada Goldenrod
Solidago canadensis
Asteraceae (Aster) Family

Commonly seen on roadsides, meadows, and open areas, Canada Goldenrod exhibits "plume-like" clusters on the tips of stems up to 4 feet tall. Leaves are long, narrow, and sharply toothed.

Canada Hawkweed
Hieracium canadense
Asteraceae (Aster) Family

Canada Hawkweed is identified by the toothed, sessile leaves ascending the stem to the floral branches. Stems may grow over 4 feet tall. Flower heads are about 1 inch in diameter.

Fringed Gentian
Gentianopsis crinita
Gentianaceae (Gentian) Family

To the Fringed Gentian

THOU blossom bright with autumn dew,
    And coloured with the heaven's own blue,
    That openest when the quiet light
    Succeeds the keen and frosty night.
Thou waitest late and com'st alone,
    When woods are bare and birds are flown,
    And frosts and shortening days portend
    The aged year is near his end.

vs 1 & 3, William Cullen Bryant

Closed or Bottle Gentian
Gentiana andrewsii
Gentianaceae (Gentian) Family

Bright blue flowers never open on Closed Gentian. Sessile, oval leaves taper to a point on stems about 1 to 2 feet in height. Habitats are similar to Spurred Gentian.

Spurred Gentian
Halenia deflexa
Gentianaceae (Gentian) Family

Greenish-colored Spurred Gentian flowers have 4 fused petals with "spurs" pointing downward. Broad leaves are sessile. It only grows about 1 to 2 feet in height. Trail sides and edges of moist woodlands are typical habitats.

Gentian in the Garden
These two Gentians are easy to grow. Bottle Gentian is especially attractive with the rich blue color in late summer.

Northern Bugleweed
Lycopus uniflorus
Lamiaceae (**Mint**) **Family**

Bugleweeds are mint-like plants in general characteristics, but their leaves do not emit a minty scent. White flowers gather tightly in the leaf axils. Notice the coarsely toothed leaf edges. Leaves taper to a long narrow point on Northern Bugleweed.

Lycopus species (not shown) differ slightly: *L. virginicus*, Virginia Bugleweed, leaves are broader, more oval. *L. americanus*, Cut-leaved or Common Water Horehound, has leaves that are more deeply cut or nearly lobed.

213

Pointed-leaved Tick-trefoil
Desmodium glutinosum
Fabaceae (Pea) Family

A long, slender, branched flower stalk rising from a short stem above a whorl of leaves is a key identifying characteristic of Pointed-leaved Tick-trefoil.

Pink to purplish pea-like flowers produce lobed pods covered with hooked hairs. When mature these hairy pods cling to clothing and fur.

Ditch Stonecrop
Penthorum sedoides
Saxifragaceae (Saxifrage) Family

At first sight, the leaves of this plant may look like Stinging Nettle (page 204). In fact, there are no stinging hairs on Ditch Stonecrop. Greenish-yellow flower clusters branch at the top of the plant. It grows 2 to 3 feet tall in wet places. Some taxonomists place **Penthorum** in the **Crassulaceae** (Sedum) Family.

Indian Tobacco
Lobelia inflata
Campanulaceae (Bluebell) Family

Notice how the base of small, light blue or white flowers becomes "inflated" as the plant matures.

This is an annual plant reproducing from seed and is reported to be the most common of all **Lobelia** species in this region. Moist, open areas are usual habitat.

Bristly Greenbrier
Smilax hispida
Smilacaceae (Greenbrier) Family

Name Change
Smilax was previously in *Liliaceae*.
It now has it's own family name.

Greenbriers are woody monocot vines. Many ***Smilax*** species are similar, most having thorns. Bristly Greenbrier is especially thorny. Umbels of small, greenish flowers appear in spring. Blue-black fruits develop over summer.

Carrion Flower
Smilax herbacea
Smilacaceae
(Greenbrier) Family

Carrion Flower is an herbaceous vine not having a woody stem. A whiff of the flowers explains its name! Look for this plant in moist woods.

Purple Virgin's Bower
Clematis verticillaris
Ranunculaceae (Buttercup) Family

Purple Virgin's Bower is a beautiful flowering vine. Its short bloom period is in early spring, making it easy to miss.

In autumn, a showy display of feathery seed heads decorates the landscape.

Another Virgin's Bower, ***C. virginiana*** (page 227) blooms later.

Having showy sepals rather than petals, Virgin's Bower is a good example of this Buttercup Family characteristic.

Fringed Bindweed
Fallopia cilinodis
Polygonaceae
(Buckwheat) Family

Loose, airy inflorescences of dainty white flowers are prolific on sprawling stems. These vines will cover shrubs, brush piles, rocks or fences. Each heart-shaped leaf has a fringed sheath surrounding the reddish stem.

Hairy Honeysuckle
Lonicera hirsuta
Caprifoliaceae (Honeysuckle) Family

Yellow to orange flowers of Hairy Honeysuckle cluster in a circular leaf collar. These flowers produce green fruits which ripen bright red.

Both of these Bindweeds belong to:
Convolvulaceae (**Morning Glory**) **Family**.

Hedge Bindweed (upper photo) has a long trailing stem with arrowhead-shaped leaves.

Low False Bindweed (lower photo) stems are short (6 to 12 inches) and have elliptical leaves.

Hedge Bindweed
Calystegia sepium

Low False Bindweed
Calystegia spithamaea

Bittersweet Nightshade
Solanum dulcamara
Solanaceae (Tomato) Family

Bittersweet Nightshade is a perennial vine, with weak stems, that is an
intrusive weed. It is recognized as being
in the tomato family with its yellow
"beak" of anthers and lavender petals
swept backward.

Bright red fruits hang in clusters all
along the vine in late summer. These
fruits have toxic substances and should
not be eaten.

Wild Yam
Dioscorea villosa
Dioscoreaceae (Yam) Family

Leaves of Wild Yam resemble those of **Smilax** (pages 216, 217), both vines being monocots. The term "yam" is often applied to certain sweet potatoes, but sweet potatoes are dicots, in the Morning Glory Family. There are some species of true yams that are grown in tropical climates for an edible tuber, but I have never seen a true yam in a grocery store in the U.S.

These Wild Yams are native temperate climate plants that thrive in moist habitats. They are native to the eastern half of the US and Canada.

male flowers

Note the thread-like male flower clusters and the 3-winged female flowers which produce the seed capsules.

In the Garden.
This is a nice vining plant for a trellis or fence. Easy to grow and available in nurseries.

seed capsules

female flowers

Hops
Humulus lupulus
Cannabaceae (Hemp) Family

Leaves of Hops are 3 to 5 lobed on long, twining vines. Some taxonomists have classified Hops and Hemp *(Canabis)* in the *Moraceae* (Mulberry) Family.

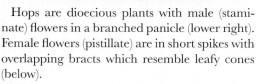

Hops are dioecious plants with male (staminate) flowers in a branched panicle (lower right). Female flowers (pistillate) are in short spikes with overlapping bracts which resemble leafy cones (below).

Hops are cultivated for the "cones" which are used as flavoring for beer.

They have escaped cultivation, naturalized and thrive in moist, open areas.

Hog Peanut
Amphicarpaea bracteata
Fabaceae (**Pea or Legume**) **Family**

These vines of deep, wooded areas produce two kinds of flowers. Pictured here are the loose clusters of pale lavender flowers that develop into 3-seeded pods.

Another flower type at the base of the stem (not pictured) is usually without petals and its pod develops with only one seed. This pod, like the peanut of commerce, may become buried underground.

225

Wild Cucumber
Echinocystis lobata
Cucurbitaceae (Squash) Family

Wild cucumber is a native annual herbaceous vine. Many tendrils enable it to climb over other plants, stumps or logs for support. It grows in wet to moist places such as stream banks and roadside ditches.

The white flowers are male or pollen flowers. Female flowers which produce spiny fruit are not showy and only a few are interspersed in the cluster.

Wild or Riverbank Grape
Vitis riparia
Vitaceae (Grape) Family

Riverbank grape is a common vine throughout the region. Earlier in the season, male flowers are present, usually on separate vines. They have withered away by the time fruits develop.

226

Old Man's Beard
or Virgin's Bower
Clematis virginiana
Ranunculaceae
(Buttercup) Family

Although they have similarities, ***Clematis virginiana*** is distinctly different from the Purple Virgin's Bower (page 218). ***C. virginiana*** blooms much later in the season.

This species has smaller flowers, each with 4 white sepals but no petals. In the fall, grayish-white, feathery seed heads look "beard-like."

227

Blueberry
Vaccinium angustifolium
Ericaceae (Heath) Family

V. angustifoium is one of several species of blueberries which produce delicious fruit.

Early white, bell-shaped, flowers are borne in small clusters. By summer, juicy, blue berries are ready for picking and become a sweet treat for bears, birds, and people.

This species grows from 1 to 2 feet high. Its shiny leaves are green on both surfaces.

Dewberry or Dwarf Raspberry
Rubus pubescens
Rosaceae (Rose) Family

Each spring, low-growing woody stems on the forest floor produce short herbaceous shoots up to 6 inches tall. White flowers give way to a cluster of fruit that looks like a red raspberry.

Because the fruit clings to its receptacle like a blackberry and does not pull away cleanly, it is technically a "dewberry." Some references name it Dwarf Raspberry.

June Berry, Serviceberry, Shadberry or Saskatoon Berry
Amelanchier spp.
Rosaceae (Rose) Family

Several species of ***Amelanchier*** are so similar they can be distinguished only by technical observations. Some references list up to 15 species. Common names given above will apply to all of this group.

Irregularly shaped white flower petals, as shown are a good representation. Appearance of flowers, slightly before the leaves fully expand, is typical growth pattern.

Pea-size fruits develop, first green, then turning reddish, finally becoming deep purple in color. These ripened fruits have a pleasant, sweet flavor.

In the Garden

Serviceberry can be attractive plants for the home landscape as well as a source of fruit production.

There is a patented cultivar, ' Autumn Brilliance' which is a hybrid of two native species. It has a vivid orange-red fall color in addition to producng quality fruit.

Chokecherry
Prunus virginiana
Rosaceae (Rose) Family

With dark green leaves, dense, elongated flower heads appear on chokecherry branches in early spring. Later, nearly black fruits develop which are astringent to taste as fresh fruit, but are delicious when made into jelly or pancake syrup!

In the Garden

There are several cultivars of Chokecherries on the market which have enhanced fall color and uniform, high quality fruit.

It is best to select these for the garden as they are propagated by grafting or cuttings to maintain the rich coloration and fruit quality.

231

Bunchberry
or Dwarf Dogwood
Cornus canadensis
Cornaceae (Dogwood) Family

Being in the Dogwood Family and having a woody rhizome, Bunchberry is shown here rather than in the herbaceous plant section. Flowers are typically Dogwood with 4 showy white bracts surrounding a cluster of tiny greenish white flowers. By mid-summer a "bunch" of bright red berries develops.

Pointed, egg-shaped leaves on this plant are limited to a single whorl of 6 on a stem about 4 to 6 inches high.

In the Garden

Excellent choice in a mass planting for a natural look in a lightly shaded landscape.

Moist, but not wet, nutrient-rich woodlands are prime habitat for Bunchberry.

Bog Rosemary
Andromeda polifolia **var.** *glaucophylla*
Ericaceae **(Heath) Family**

Grows in cold bogs. Low growing reaching barely 2 feet. Narrow evergreen leaves with edges rolled under are whitish on the underside. Pinkish-white flowers are in pendant clusters near the top of the stem

Bog Gardens
Water and bog features are gaining popularity. There are many attractive plants available to make a spectacular show in the landscape.

More are listed on pp. 236-238. On proir pages, several orchids have been illustrated as well as Buckbean, p 45, Pitcher Plant, p. 98, and Sundew, p. 155. Any or all of these are good choices for a bog.

Leatherleaf
Chamaedaphne calyculata
Ericaceae **(Heath) Family**

Grows in cold bogs along with Bog Rosemary.

Stiff, leathery leaves are evergreen with minute rusty colored scales on the underside. White vase-shaped flowers form in the leaf axils and dangle in a row beneath the branches.

Pin Cherry
Prunus pensylvanica
Rosaceae (Rose) Family

Pin Cherry flowers appear as a "ready-made" corsage on the leafy branches of this small tree. Shiny red fruits develop mid-summer.

In the Garden
Like other Prunus genera, the Pin Cherry is useful in the home landscape. These fruits are sour to taste but make excellent jelly and wine.

Fly Honeysuckle
Lonicera canadensis
Caprifoliaceae (Honeysuckle) Family

Fly Honeysuckle plants are small shrubs about 3 feet in height. Greenish-white flowers come in pairs and produce unique sets of red berries. Ripened berries don't last long as they are relished by birds.

A later blooming Honeysuckle (*Diervilla lonicera*, Northern Bush Honeysuckle) is pictured on page 240.

Labrador Tea
Rhododendron groenlandicum
Ericaceae (Heath) Family

Labrador Tea are small shrubs which grow in cold bogs. They brighten the landscape in spring with a flush of white 5-petaled blossoms.

Leaves, typically rolled on the edges, have a brownish wool on the underside.

Capsules develop that have a prominent beak.

Thriving in a cold bog along with white flowering Labrador Tea, Swamp Laurel highlights the scene with color. Narrow, elliptical, leathery leaves have edges rolled downward.

Being a shrubby plant, it stands about 2 feet high. Red fruits become brown at maturation.

Pale or Swamp Laurel
Kalmia polifolia
Ericaceae (Heath) Family

237

Small Cranberry
Vaccinium oxycoccus
Ericaceae (Heath) Family

A miniature version of Large Cranberry, ***V. macrocarpon***, the "Thanksgiving" cranberry, Small Cranberry inhabits wet Sphagnum Moss bogs. Dainty flowers rise up just a few inches from trailing stems followed by small fruits as in the photo shown right.

The yellow arrow below points to a cinnamon-colored spore capsule of Sphagnum Moss.

Sand Cherry
Prunus pumila
Rosaceae (**Rose**) **Family**

Sand Cherry is at home on sandy dunes and beaches of the Great Lakes. A shrubby plant, it may grow 2 to 3 feet tall. Its branches become profusely covered with white blossoms in spring followed by marble-size, deep purple fruits.

These fruits will "pucker" your mouth when eaten fresh, but are fine made into jelly.

Northern Bush Honeysuckle
Diervilla lonicera
Caprifoliaceae (Honeysuckle) Family

Clusters of 2 to 6 funnel-shaped yellow flowers are usually located at the branch tips of Northern Bush Honeysuckle. Unlike other honeysuckles, it has leaves with serrated margins. This bushy shrub reaches 1 to 4 feet in height.

In the Garden
Northern Bush Honeysuckle makes an excellent choice as a landscape shrub. It keeps a compact shape, leaves are attractive and has delicate flowers. It grows well in a wide range of soils and light conditions.

Bearberry
Arctostaphylos uva-ursi
Ericaceae (Heath) Family

Bearberry is a sprawling plant of short upright shoots on a trailing woody stem. Leaves are leathery and evergreen. Tiny vase-shaped flowers hang in clusters. Red berries develop by mid-summer and unless eaten, remain through the winter.

Highbush Cranberry
Viburnum trilobum
Adoxaceae (Mochatel) Family

Highbush Cranberry has no relationship to the "Thanksgiving" cranberry which is in the Heath Family. Highbush is a large shrub 3 to 9 feet tall.

Large sterile (without stamen or pistil) flowers form a ring surrounding smaller, fertile, fruit-producing flowers in the center of the inflorescence. Pea-size fruits, which ripen in summer, are sour to taste but delicious as jelly or syrup.

> ### *Viburnum*
> ### in the Garden
> ***V. trilobum*** along with several other ***Viburnum*** species are useful landscape shrubs.

Shrubby Cinquefoil
Dasiphora fruticosa
Rosaceae (Rose) Family

This native shrub is one of the most versatile plants in the country. It thrives on this rocky ledge along Lake Superior, but it has also become a mainstay of landscape planting in home gardens and commercial developments.

In adverse conditions like the rocky crevice, it may get only 1 foot high, but in good soil, this shrub will reach 4 feet in height.

Prickly Gooseberry
Ribes cynosbati
Grossulariaceae (Gooseberry) Family

Name Change
Gooseberries and Currants or the genus ***Ribes*** has been in ***Saxifragaceae*** or **Saxifrage Family**. They are now listed in ***Grossulariaceae*** or **Gooseberry Family**

Ribes is the genus of Gooseberries and Currants, another group of similar species throughout this region.

Basically, gooseberries have prickles on their stems. In contrast, currant stems are usually smooth.

Prickly Gooseberry is a small shrub growing about 3 feet tall. Its flowers have 5 fused petals forming a bell-like center surrounded by 5 greenish-white sepals

243

Skunk Currant
Ribes glandulosum
Grossulariaceae (**Gooseberry**) **Family**

Skunk Currant flowers are small in comparison to Prickly Gooseberry (page 243), and its 5 petals are distinctly separate.

What's in a name? This Currant has a distinct odor: The leaves smell like "skunk" when bruised and the fruits are so bad tasting, birds avoid them.

Wild Rose
Rosa spp.
Rosaceae (Rose) Family

Several species of native wild roses, in a variety of habitats, are abundant in this region. Species differences are subtle, such as the size and shape of the pointed, dried sepals on the hips (fruits) shown left. The sepals on the red hips all point outward but on the green hips the sepals flatten in a star-like pattern. Another species difference is in number, size, shape, and location of prickles or thorns along the stem, while others have smooth stems.

Most have flowers that are variations of pink, but white or yellow also occur. Flowers range in size less than 1 inch to over 3 inches across. All have compound leaves, but leaflet number varies from 3 to 11 from species to species.

In the Garden

There are hundreds of species of Roses from all over the world. With hybridization, there are countless variations, but the old fasioned wild rose in the forests still has it's beauty.

Mountain Ash
Sorbus americana
Rosaceae (Rose) Family

Taxonomists differ in classifying Mountain Ash. Some place it in genus **Pyrus**, the genus of pears.

Another Mountain Ash, **S. decora** (not shown) is almost identical, but has larger fruit and slightly shorter leaflets.

A non-native species, **S. aucuparia,** is also sold in nurseries. It is reported that the European species is somewhat susceptible to fire blight.

In the Garden
This Mountain Ash is often used as a landscape specimen. The blossoms in the spring are followed by an attractive show of orange to red berries.

Readily available in nurseries.

Red-osier Dogwood
Cornus stolonifera
Cornaceae (Dogwood) Family

Red-osier Dogwood spreads by stolons, forming dense thickets up to 8 feet or more. Young stems are reddish in color.

Clusters of white, 4-petaled flowers are flat-topped, about 2 inches across. Ripened berries resemble White Baneberry fruits (p. 22).

In the Garden

This plant, along with other Dogwood species, is often used in landscaping as an ornamental shrub.

Readily available in nurseries.

Ninebark
Physocarpus opulifolius
Rosaceae (Rose) Family

A large shrub up to 9 feet in height, Ninebark gives a showy display of rosy-pink buds before opening to white or pinkish flowers. Many stamens give a soft brush-like appearance to the open flowers.

Stems have bark that splits and peals off in strips with age and weathering.

Ninebark has become commercially available for landscape use.

Thimbleberry or Flowering Raspberry
Rubus parviflorus
Rosaceae (Rose) Family

What these raspberries lack in succulent, sweet flavor, they make up in a spring display of showy white flowers. Fruits, quite edible when ripe, taste more tart than common red raspberries.

Large leaves, up to 8 inches across, have likeness to Maple leaves. Stems are without thorns and grow 3 to 6 feet high.

Meadowsweet
Spirea alba
Rosaceae (Rose) Family

White to pinkish flowers on a branched, spiraling inflorescence give Meadowsweet a distinctive look. Numerous protruding stamens make the flowers appear "woolly."

Stems are brownish and grow 2 to 6 feet high. Lance-shaped leaves are sharply toothed.

S. latifolia (not shown), a similar Meadowsweet, has wider, more coarsely-toothed leaves on a reddish to purple-brown stem. It is more common in the eastern part of the region, while *S. alba* is more prevalent in the western Great Lakes area.

Speckled Alder
Alnus rugosa

Speckled Alder flowers are borne in catkins. Both male (white arrow) and female (red arrow) catkins are on the same plant. These develop in the previous season and pollination occurs in spring before leaves appear. Seed forms in cone-like structures, as below (yellow arrow), releasing seed in fall. Woody "cones" remain similar to the cones on conifers.

Alder and Hazel are in *Betulaceae* (Birch) Family

Beaked Hazel
Corylus cornuta

Female flowers on Beaked Hazel have only bright red stigmas of the flower exposed to receive pollen from the pendulous male catkins. Curious Beaked Hazel fruits have sticky, fuzzy husks containing a round "filbert" or Hazelnut.

Ripened Hazelnuts are soon harvested and stored away by hungry squirrels.

Swamp Dewberry
Rubus spp.
Rosaceae (Rose) Family

Growing on peat land, this Dewberry is well-dressed in springtime with sparkling white flowers. It is a short, sprawling shrub standing only 1 to 2 feet high. Ripened fruit are purple-to-black by the end of summer.

Blackberry
Rubus spp.
Rosaceae (Rose) Family

Blackberry thickets thrive in the forests of the Great Lakes region. There are several species, most of which can be recognized by white flowers, rambling, prickly canes, and delicious purple-black berries that ripen by late summer.

Red Elderberry
Sambucus racemosa
Adoxaceae
(Mochatel) Family

Walter Siegmund

Name Change

The ***Sambucus*** genus has recently been moved from ***Caprifoliaceae*** (Honeysuckle) Family to ***Adoxaceae***.

Red Elderberry stands out in woodlands when large panicle-like bunches of red fruits command attention. These shrubs grow to 9 feet tall in moist woods.

The spring bloom is also a show with the large white inflorescence.

Sweet Gale
Myrica gale
Myricaceae (Wax-myrtle) Family

Sweet Gale is at home in bogs and shallow ponds of woodlands around the Great Lakes. It is a small shrub growing to about four feet tall. The leaves give off an aroma when crushed, hence it's name.

Flowers are catkins on leafless terminal twigs, usually on separate plants. Red female catkins are very similar to those of Beaked Hazel on page 251.

Male catkins

Female catkins

255

Grasses and Sedges

Sedges are sometimes described as "grass-like." Although they have similarities, these plants are in separate Families. Sedges are in the **Cyperaceae** Family. Grasses belong to **Poaceae** (also called **Graminae**). The two families, because of their similarities, belong to a higher level of classification (Order) called **Poales**. Common characteristics of **Poales** include blade-like leaves and flowers without petals or sepals.

Grasses have jointed, circular, and usually hollow stems. Most grasses prefer drier habitats.

Sedges have triangular, solid stems that are not jointed. They normally thrive in wet places.

Tussock Cottongrass
Eriophorum vaginatum
Cyperaceae (Sedge) Family

Soft, thread-like hairs mimicking cotton bolls at harvest in the South, cover the seed head of this sedge in the summer. This Cottongrass grows in a bog environment.

Several species are found in the Great Lakes region with their range extending into the tundra of northern Canada and Alaska.

Carex Sedge
Carex intumescens
Cyperaceae (Sedge) Family

Carex species are monoecious, like corn, having pollen-forming flowers in tassels while seed forming flowers are in "ears."

Carex pollen develops in a brown spike (yellow arrows). Seeds ripen in the inflated, pointed green flowers (red arrow).

Carex Sedge
Carex comosa
Cyperaceae (Sedge) Family

Hard Stem Bulrush
Scirpus acutus
Cyperaceae (Sedge) Family

Bulrush
Scirpus spp.
Cyperaceae (Sedge) Family

Bulrush species are many and hard to identify. This group thrives in wet places, even in standing water of ponds and lake shores. Some have leaves that closely resemble grasses and others look more like reeds.

Wild or Foxtail Barley
Hordeum jubatum
Poaceae (Grass) Family

Wild Barley is a perennial grass in the same genus as the barley of commerce.

Many road sides become lined with the soft, purplish-green "foxtail" seed heads in summer. It also thrives in meadows and waste places.

It is native to all states except the southeastern continental states and Hawaii.

Pennsylvania Sedge
Carex pensylvanica
Cyperaceae (Sedge)
Family

In the Garden

Pennsylvania Sedge may have a place as a ground cover in a woodland landscape. It naturalizes in woodlands where other plants have died out, especially due to invasion by European earthworms

Earthworms eat fallen leaves which reduces the amount of naturally decaying organic matter.

Many native wildflowers developed without earthworms.

Timothy
Phleum pratense
Poaceae (Grass) Family

Timothy, named Meadow Cat's Tail elsewhere, is a perennial found growing in meadows and road ditches. Like a small bottle brush, the cylindrical, green flower head has a unique appearance.

It is an introduced species for use as a pasture and hay crop.

Smooth Brome Grass
Bromus inermis
Poaceae (Grass) Family

These flowers of **B. inermis** hang in loose panicles. Dry, open meadows and road sides are common habitat where this grass has become naturalized.

Smooth Brome Grass, brought **from Europe**, is cultivated extensively for pasture and hay.

Reed Canary Grass
Phalaris arundinacea
Poaceae (Grass) Family

Common to wet, meadow-like areas, Reed Canary Grass grows aggressively once established. This native grass is coarse stemmed and tall (up to 6 feet).

"Ribbon Grass" and "Gardener's Garters" are names given to variations that have white stripes running the length of the leaves.

Canary Grass In the Garden

Striped variations make handsome landscape plants, especially in areas where their invasive tendencies will not become a problem.

Ferns, Clubmosses and Horsetails

What's not blooming? Ferns, Club mosses and Horsetails are plants without flowers and seeds, but they also have their place in the "wild" world. They are set apart because their sexual reproductive cycle is completed without the formation of a seed.

Visible reproductive structures of these plants produce spores on the underside of leaves (fronds) in Ferns or in "cones" at the tip of a stalk as with Horsetails and Club mosses. These spores continue the reproductive process, forming an inconspicuous intermediate generation in which sperm and egg are formed and join to complete the life cycle of these unique plants.

Natures Garden

We can learn from nature on designing our own landscapes. Hiking through the woodlands and taking stock of the plants that share the same habitat, the soil type, amount of shade versus sunshine and the relative amount of water available will give a clue of what plants you might choose. My advice "mimic nature".

Fern Fiddleheads

Fiddleheads or crosiers are the beginning of fern leaves called fronds. Fronds begin to grow on underground stems (rhizomes). They poke through the soil, coiled like the scroll of a fiddle and come in many shapes and sizes depending on species.

Name Changes in Ferns

Fern names have been shuffled around as have the flowering plants. See the discussion on page 286.

Ferns in the Garden

Most native woodland ferns are attractive additions to a landscape and are quite easy to establish and maintain. Bracken and Ostrich ferns are somewhat invasive and it may be wise to avoid those.

Non-invasive ferns include Berry Bladder, Leatherwood, Cinnamon, Sensitive, Interupted Male, Lady, Royal and Maidenhair.

Royal and Maidenhair deserve special mention as their leaf structure has more individual character bringing unique texture into a landscape.

Berry or Bulblet Bladder Fern
Cystopteris bulbifera
Dryopteridaceae (Wood Fern) Family

    The Berry name is derived from a small green bulblet (left) that forms on the underside of the stipe (leaf stalk). This is a means of vegetative reproduction as these bulblets form new plants when dropped to moist soil. White spots that appear on the underside of the pinules are sori where spores are produced for sexual reproduction.

Male Fern
Dryopteris felix-mas
Dryopteridaceae (Wood Fern) Family

Northern Maidenhair Fern
Adiantum pedatum
Pteridaceae (Maidenhair) Family

Lacy fronds of Maidenhair Fern make an attractive accompaniment to Large-flowered Trillium blossoms. These delicate-looking fronds form a fan-shaped pattern which makes them easy to recognize. Height may vary from 12 to 18 inches.

Like most ferns, *A. pedatum* keeps good form from spring to fall. The rich fall color, shown below, is an added attraction.

Cinnamon Fern
Osmundastrum cinnamomeum
Osmundaceae (Royal Fern) Family

Cinnamon and Royal Ferns have two types of fronds. Narrow, erect fertile fronds begin green, but soon wither and turn to a cinnamon-brown as the spores form. Sterile fronds are wider and longer (up to 3 feet long), arching outward and remain green through the summer.

Ferns in *Osmundaceae* are often referred to as the Flowering ferns

Royal Fern
Osmunda regalis
Osmundaceae (Royal Fern) Family

LadyFern
Athyrium felix-femina
Dryopteridaceae
(**Wood Fern**) **Family**

Sori (spore producing structures) developing on the underside of Ladyfern pinules. The "eyebrow" shape is a distinguishing characteristic of Lady ferns.

Ostrich Fern
Matteuccia struthiopteris
Onocleaceae
(Sensitive Fern) Family

Ostrich Fern is perhaps the tallest of the temperate climate ferns with fronds growing 5 to 6 feet tall

Although most often described as clump forming, they do spread by rhizomes quite rapidly in a garden setting.

The fiddle heads (younger than those pictured) are used as a green vegetable. There are reports of people becoming ill from eating raw fiddle heads. It is recommended they be cooked thoroughly before eating.

Sensitive Fern or Bead Fern
Onoclea sensibilis
Onocleaceae (Sensitive fern) Family
Formerly in *Polypodiaceae* (Polypody) Family

Sensitive to cold, green fronds of this fern rapidly turn brown with the first frost of autumn. Sterile fronds with large leaflets are the most prominent, being 2 feet tall. Brownish fertile fronds turn purplish-black by fall, (right). They remain nearly hidden among the taller sterile fronds. The 'bead-like" structures are where the spores are produced.

These ferns grow in a wide range of habitats, from full sun to shade and wet to dry soils.

Interrupted Fern
Osmunda claytoniana
Osmundaceae (Royal Fern) Family

Fertile fronds, also the tallest fronds, stand upright in *O. claytoniana*. Spore-producing pinnae (leaflets) are located only on the central part of the frond, "interrupting" the pattern of green sterile leaflets. Sterile fronds without brown leaflets are shorter and bend outward. These ferns thrive in shaded woodlands as well as full sun environments.

Spore Producing Pinnae

271

Rattlesnake Fern
Botrichium virginianum

Mingan Moonwort
Botrichium minganense

Joshua Horky

Little Grape Fern
Botrichium simplex

Joshua Horky

These three ferns are an oddity because they all have one stalk which divides into two fronds. A lacy, green, sterile frond spreads out like a fan. The other is a fertile frond that projects upward. Once the fertile frond produces spores, it withers and disappears.

Moist, shaded woodlands are home to these species.

All are in ***Botrychiaceae*** **(Moonwort) Family**

Bracken Fern
Pteridium aquilinum
Dennstaedtiaceae (**Bracken Fern**) **Family**

Bracken Fern crozier

Joshua Horky

Formerly in *Polypodiaceae* (**Polypody**) **Family**

Bracken Ferns, one of the most common ferns, are invasive and form large colonies in open sunny areas or in light shade. Fronds grow 3 feet tall. Spores are produced in lines on the underside of the leaflets. Young fiddleheads are eaten in some cultures, the mature fronds are toxic to farm animals.

273

Marginal Wood Fern aka
Eastern Wood or **Leather Wood Fern.**
Dryopteris marginalis
Dryopteridaceae
(Wood Fern) Family

Marginal Wood Fern in the Garden
The leathery leaves of Dryopteris marginalis are a beautiful addition to a woodland garden. It forms a lovely and easy to maintain groundcover.

Marginal Wood Fern forms a nice clump that will not spread and is very tolerant of dry shady conditions once established.

Rock or Common Polypody Fern
Polypodium virginianum
Polypodiaceae (Polypody) Family

Rock Polypody Ferns are evergreen, even in harsh northern winters. As the name implies, crevices in rocks are a favorite habitat. Rusty-colored sporangia appear on the under side of the fronds, ready to disperse their spores to start a new generation of ferns.

Forest Horsetail
Equisetum sylvaticum
Equisetaceae (Horsetail) Family

Forest Horsetail is a "bushy" horsetail with whorls of branches spreading outward from joints in the stem. The "fertile" stems in the photo have spore cones at the tips. Sterile stems (shown below) do not have cones and their whorls branch 2 or 3 times, creating a plume-like appearance.

Other *Equisetum* species, lacking whorls of branches, are called Scouring Rush because their stems are rough with silica and feel like sandpaper.

Circeus

275

Running or Staghorn Clubmoss
Lycopodium clavatum
Lycopodiaceae (Clubmoss) Family

Running Clubmoss is evergreen with horizontal stems creeping over the surface of the ground. Upright stems branch, supporting "cones" at the tips.

Inky Cap Mushroom
Coprinus comatus

Mushrooms like the ferns are not really blooming. However, the mushroom cap is the spore producing body which produces the reproductive cells and they can be an interesting find along a wildflower hike.

More interesting and beautiful mushrooms. This is not intended to be a mushroom book, but they are intriguing. To discover while searching for photo opts along the woodland trails, stopping to take a picture is a must.

Red Waxcap Mushroom
Hygrocybe coccinea

Fly Agaric Mushroom (left)
Amanita muscaria

Beautiful mushroom, but this one is poisonous.

Pixie Cup Lichen
Cladonia chlorophaea

See page 278 for information about Lichens

British Soldiers

British Soldiers, ***Cladonia cristatella,*** are Lichens. Lichens are a combination of two organisms, algae and fungi, growing together. Algae are green, containing chlorophyll, allowing photosynthesis for sugar (food) production. Fungi do not have chlorophyll, but feed from the algae. In turn, the fungi provides minerals and a moist environment for the algae. Red tops are reproductive structures which appear in springtime.

Orchid Gallery

**Collection of photos
by
Josh Horky
pages 279 -284**

The Orchids in Mr. Horky's collection were photographed in Pictured Rock National Park, Michigan; Apostle Islands National Lakeshore, Wisconsin and other Natural areas in Minnesota, Wisconsin and Michigan.

Round-leaved Orchis
Amerorchis rotundifolia
Orchidaceae Family

Fairy Lady's-slipper
Calypso bulbosa **var.**
americana
Orchidaceae **Family**

Broad-leaved Twayblade
Listera convallarioides
Orchidaceae Family

Heart-leaved Twayblade
Listera cordata
Orchidaceae Family

Lily-leaved Twayblade
Liparis lilifolia
Orchidaceae Family

Striped Coral Root
Corallorhiza striata
Orchidaceae Family

Early Coral Root
Corallorhiza trifida
Orchidaceae Family

PLANT FAMILY FACTS
A Few Common Traits

Flower structure is a major determining factor for sorting plants into families. Structure of the flower includes: 1) counting parts in each whorl, such as the number of sepals, petals, stamens and carpels; and 2) detail of the position of these parts, one to another, such as fusing of petals to form a bell. Leaf arrangement, stem characteristics and even root structure aid in placement of plants into categories.

Plant identification is a fascinating study. I recommended *Taxonomy of Flowering Plants by Porter* or *Manual of Vascular Plants of Northeastern United States and Adjacent Canada* by Gleason and Cronquist in my previous edition of *What's Doin' the Bloomin'?*. These references remain useful resources for readers interested in learning more about recognizing and grouping plants into families; however, many name changes have occurred since these books were published.

Botanical names are governed by the International Code of Botanical Nomenclature. Family names are usually recognized by the suffix *"aceae"* attached to the stem of one genus name within the family. There are eight family names of Angiosperms that were historically given an *"ae"* ending. Traditionally they are still used. In this edition of *What's Doin' the Bloomin'?* (guide), both the International Code Rule (Family Name) and traditional name are listed.

The traditional name of the Sunflower Family, was the Compositae Family which included all of the disk flowers like sunflowers, asters, dandelions, daisies and seemingly countless others. The Sunflower Family (*Compositae* Family) was changed to *Asteraceae* Family. This follows the rule that one genus would have the stem of the family name. The genus *Aster* became the genus of choice.

Since the advent of DNA analysis of chromosomes, plant relationships can be determined by DNA tests which requires a reshuffling of plant names. The Lily Family (*Liliaceae*) illustrates significant changes in plant names and relationships. You will note that many of the plants throughout this book, formerly listed as being in the Lily family, now have new names.

A helpful references related to DNA analysis of chromosomes and plant relationships is:
http://en.wikipedia.org/wiki/Angiosperm_Phylogeny_Group

The following Plant Family list reflects changes from the previous edition of *What's Doin' the Bloomin'?*

ANGIOSPERMS

ANGIOSPERM is the term given to all **flowering, seed producing plants**. This category is divided again into two groups: MONOCOTS and DICOTS. Monocots have 1 cotyledon (embryonic leaf) in their seeds, flower parts in 3's or multiples of 3 and blade-like leaves with parallel veins. Dicots have 2 cotyledons, flower parts usually in 4's or 5's. Leaves show a netted vein pattern.

MONOCOTS

Alismataceae (Arrowhead)
Wetland herbaceous plants with arrow-, lance- or oval-shaped leaves. Flower parts in whorls of 3. Petals usually white.

Amaryllidaceae (Amaryllis)
Similar to Liliaceae except the sepals and petals are attached above the ovary (epigynous) rather than below (hypogynous).

Araceae (Arum or Calla)
Flowers bloom atop a spike-like structure called a spadix, surrounded by a leaf-like spathe. Tropical genera in this family include Philodendron, Anthurium and Monstera (Split-leaf Philodendron) and are grown as houseplants.

Cyperaceae (Sedge)
Herbaceous plants resembling grasses, but stems are not jointed and are usually triangular in cross section. Flowers lack petals but may have

bristles or hairs instead. A bract called a glume or scale covers the flower.

Dioscoreaceae (Yam)

Flowers have 3 sepals and 3 petals which look alike (tepals) and 6 stamens. Vining plants, Yams have heart-shaped leaves growing up from thick rhizomes or tubers. Most Yams are tropical, but Dioscorea villosa is native to this region. Red, orange or yellow "yams" marketed in grocery stores are really "sweet potatoes", members of Convolvulaceae (Morning Glory Family).

Iridaceae (Iris)

Rhizome or corm producing. Parallel-veined leaves fold lengthwise around the stem at their base. Flower parts in whorls of 3.

Liliaceae (Lily)

Parallel-veined leaves. Flower parts in multiples of 3. Sepals often colored and shaped like petals. Petals usually bell-shaped. Plants often form bulbs.

Orchidaceae (Orchid)

Flower parts in whorls of 3. Sepals often petaloid (petal-like). Two lateral petals with a larger third petal forming a pouch, sac or lip-like structure. Leaves parallel-veined. Orchid species are found from arctic to tropical regions. Most temperate region Orchids are terrestrial (grow in soil). Tropical species tend to be epiphytic (growing on tree branches and taking nourishment from the air and water).

Poaceae or *Gramineae* (Grass)

Mostly herbaceous plants with jointed stems, usually hollow between the joints. Flowers lack sepals and petals. 3 or 6 stamens and a pistil are between two scales called the lemma and palea. Other bracts called glumes may surround the flower. Fruit in grasses is a grain where the ovary wall is fused to the seed coat, like a corn kernel. Some of the largest grasses include corn and bamboo.

Typhaceae (Cattail)

Wetland herbaceous plants with ridged stems and long, blade-like leaves. Tiny male and female flowers bloom separately on a spike at the stem tip.

DICOTS

Anacardiaceae (Sumac or Cashew)

Mostly tropical trees and shrubs. Cashew, Mango

and Pistachio trees are widely known for their delicious fruits. Our temperate climate Sumac, Poison Ivy and Poison Oak are in this family. Both temperate and tropical family members have toxic parts. Structures of reproductive parts in flowers put all these plants in the same family group.

Apiaceae or *Umbelliferae* (Parsley)

Inflorescence usually a flat-topped umbel. Often referred to as Carrot, Celery, Dill, or Parsnip Family.

Apocynaceae (Dogbane)

Herbaceous or woody plants. Flower parts in whorls of 5. Petals fused to form a bell shape. Stems have a milky juice. Several tropical species including Plumeria and Oleander are well known. Several species are toxic.

Araliaceace (Ginseng)

Small flowers usually bloom in a round umbel. Compound leaves either alternate or in 3's.

Aristolochiaceae (Birthwort)

Although most in this family are tropical, Wild Ginger is not. Flowers have 3 purple-brown, petal-like sepals flaring out like a cup. Leaves are heart-shaped. Dutchman's Pipe is another example of this family.

Asclepiadaceae (Milkweed)

Five-part flower whorls with the sepals and petals curving backwards. Another set of appendages arise from the petals or the stamens, forming a petal-like "corona." Stems have a milky juice.

Asteraceae or Compositae (Aster)

Often called Sunflower or Daisy Family, this is the largest family of plants numbering thousands of species in a broad range of habitats. Porter reports about 950 genera and 20,000 species. The largest genus, Senecio, has about 2,300 species alone. Many small flowers, in dense heads, appear as one flower like Asters and Sunflowers. This dense flower formation is the key structural characteristic. Often a ring of ray flowers with showy petals surrounds a central disk of minute, seed-producing, disk flowers. Others have only disk flowers or only ray flowers.

Balsaminaceae (Touch-me-not)

Succulent stems, thin leaves and irregular-shaped flowers. Most are tropical, such as the Impatiens used as annual bedding plants. Ripe seedpods coil and spring open when touched, forcefully ejecting their seeds.

Berberidaceae (Barberry)

Mostly woody shrubs but there are 3 herbaceous genera in our area, Podophyllum (May Apple), Jeffersonia (Twinleaf), and Caulophyllum (Blue Cohosh). Flower parts in 4 or 6.

Betulaceae (Birch)

A family of trees and shrubs. Flowers are usually in the form of catkins (pendulous spikes of diminutive flowers) which bear only male or female flowers.

Boraginaceae (Borage)

Mostly bristly, hairy, herbaceous plants. Five fused petals form a tube on which the stamens are attached. Inflorescence usually coiled, unrolling as it grows.

Brassicaceae or Cruciferae (Mustard)

Flowers with 4 petals and normally 6 stamens. Ovary 2-celled, forming a long, narrow, pod-like fruit (silique).

Campanulaceae (Bluebell)

Flower parts in 5's. Petals fused in the form of a bell. Stamens normally free standing.

Cannabinaceae (Hemp)

Plants are herbaceous, either vining or erect. Male and female flowers are usually on separate plants. Female flowers are without petals and in bract-like spikes. Male flowers are in panicles, each flower having 5 sepals and 5 stamens. Only 2 genera, Cannabis (Hemp) and Humulus (Hops) are in this family. Some taxonomists place them in Moraceae (Mulberry Family) and others in Urticaceae (Nettle Family).

Caprifoliaceae (Honeysuckle)

Most are woody shrubs or vines. Flowers with 5 parts per whorl. Petals are fused, with stamens attached to the petals. Twinflower is an exception to the woody characteristic of the family.

Caryophyllaceae (Pink)

Flowers usually have notched petals, some looking like they have been cut with "pinking" shears, hence their name "Pink." Pinks come in many colors. Flower parts in whorls of 5 (sometimes 4). Stems have swollen joints.

Cistaceae (Rockrose)

Low-growing plants with crowded, scale-like leaves. Flowers have 5 petals which age and fall quickly. Many stamens.

Convolvulaceae (Morning-glory)

Herbaceous plants, many with vining growth habit. Tubular or funnel-shaped flowers with 5 fused petals. Genus Cuscuta (Dodder) is a parasitic weed.

Cornaceae (Dogwood)

Mostly trees and shrubs with the exception of Bunchberry. Small flowers have parts in 4's. Inflorescence may be surrounded by showy bracts as in Flowering Dogwood or Bunchberry.

Droseraceae (Sundew)

Small, insectivorous plants of bogs. Leaves are spoon-shaped in a rosette. Flowers on a slender stalk have 5 petals.

Ericaceae (Heath)

Flower parts in 4's or 5's. Petals often fused to form a bell shape. Mostly woody shrubs, but also low-growing forms such as Bearberry.

Fabaceae or Leguminosae (Pea or Legume)

Another large family. Flowers are irregular (will divide into mirror images only if cut in one direction). Five petals with 2 fused enclosing the pistil; 2 form "wings" to the sides and one forms a larger "banner" over the top of the flower. Fruit is a legume or pod.

Fumariaceae (Fumitory)

See Papaveraceae.

Gentianaceae (Gentian)

Flower parts in 4's or 5's with petals fused together and stamens attached to the corolla (fused whorl of petals).

Geraniaceae (Geranium)

Flower parts in whorls of 5. Pistil has a beak-like structure called a "cranes bill" which splits away into 5 curled strips, each containing 1 or 2 seeds.

Hydrophyllaceae (Waterleaf)

Flower parts in 5's. Petals fused into a bell shape. Stamens often long and extend beyond the edge of the petals. Leaves often have spots which look like "water spots."

Hypericaceae (St. Johns'-wort)

Herbaceous or shrubby plants. Leaves often with dots. Yellow flowers. Flower parts in 3's or 5's.

Lamiaceae or **Labiatae** (Mint)

Aromatic herbaceous plants. Stems square. Small flowers with 5 petals irregular in shape. Two long and 2 short stamens; a fifth stamen either absent or smaller and infertile.

Lentibulariaceae (Bladderwort)

Mostly insectivorous water plants. Submerged leaves have "bladders" which trap small aquatic animals for a source of nutrients. Flowers have 2 "lips" nearly the same as Scrophulariaceae.

Lythraceae (Loosestrife)

Flowers with 3 to 6 petals are often purple, in terminal clusters. Narrow, upright growth pattern. (Different from yellow-flowered Loosestrife plants, members of the Primrose Family.)

Malvaceae (Mallow)

Flower parts in multiples of 5. Stamens cluster around the pistil as in Hibiscus and Hollyhocks.

Nymphaeaceae (Water Lily)

Plants root in mud at the bottom of shallow lakes and ponds. Flower stalks arise from the base of the plants. Leaves float flat on the water surface.

Onagraceae (Evening Primrose)

Flower parts in whorls of 4 (some in 2's). Seeds often have tufts of hairs allowing wind dispersal.

Oxalidaceae Wood Sorrel)

Juice of the plant is sour, containing oxalic acid. Compound leaves have 3 heart-shaped leaflets. Flower parts in whorls of 5.

Papaveraceae (Poppy)

Milky juice in stem. Flower parts in multiples of 4. Numerous stamens. Lobed leaves. Corydalis and Dicentra, included in this family, are placed in Fumeriaceae by some taxonomists.

Plantaginaceae (Plantain)

Non-showy flowers on a slender stalk arising from the crown of the plant. Leaves in a basal rosette.

Polemoniaceae (Phlox)

Flower parts in 5's. Fused petals form a tube. Stamens partially fused to the petals (corolla).

Polygalaceae (Milkwort)

Flower parts irregular, like legumes. One example illustrated here is Polygala.

Polygonaceae (Buckwheat)

Stems with swollen joints. Tiny flowers are without petals and clustered on a spike-like stem tip. Sepals may be colored.

Pontederiaceae (Water Hyacinth)

A small family of water plants, mostly growing in shallow water. Propagation by rhizomes makes them form large colonies.

Portulacaceae (Purslane)

Flowers with 2 sepals and usually 5 petals. Leaves tend to be thick and succulent. An exception, Spring Beauty, has thin leaves.

Primulaceae (Primrose)

Flower parts in whorls of 5. Stamens attached to the center of petals. Evening Primrose plants are in the Onagraceae (Evening Primrose) Family, not in the Primrose Family. Confusing?

Pyrolaceae (Pyrola or Wintergreen)

Small, basically evergreen, woodland plants. Flower parts in whorls of 5. Some taxonomists consider this a subfamily of Ericaceae (Heath Family).

Ranunculaceae (Buttercup or Crowfoot)

Flower parts highly variable in number. Three to many sepals that may be petal-like. Certain species lack petals. Commonly many stamens and pistils form a "button" in the flower center.

Rosaceae (Rose)

Flower parts in multiples of 5. Numerous stamens. A large family including most of the temperate climate fruits such as apples, pears, peaches, plums, raspberries, and strawberries.

Rubiaceae (Madder or Bedstraw)

Mostly tree or shrubs (including Coffee and Gardenia) in tropical regions. In this temperate climate, there are small herbaceous species. Flower parts usually in whorls of 4. Petals fused with stamens attached

Santalaceae (Sandalwood)

A group of parasitic plants that attach to other species to draw nourishment, especially early in their development. Flowers have 5 sepals, no petals and 5 stamens. Mostly tropical.

Sarraceniaceae (Pitcher Plant)

Insectivorous plants with tubular leaves that collect water and insects. Flower stalks arise from the base of the plants. Flower parts in whorls of 5. Style on pistil forms an umbrella shape.

Saxifragaceae (Saxifrage)

Flowers resemble those of the Rose Family. Leaves usually form a rosette. Flower parts in 4's or 5's

Scrophulariaceae (Snapdragon or Figwort)

Flower parts in whorls of 5. Unequal petals fused into a tube often with lobes forming an upper and lower "lip." Five stamens fused to petals, usually 4 fertile and 1 sterile.

Solanaceae (Tomato or Nightshade)

Also known as Potato or Tobacco Family. Mostly herbaceous, but occasionally woody. Some are vines such as Bittersweet Nightshade. Flower parts in 5's. Stamens attached to fused petals. Several species have toxic substances.

Urticaceae (Nettle)

Often have stinging hairs on stems and leaves. Flowers are inconspicuous on string-like racemes coming from leaf axils.

Valerianaceae (Valerian)

Fused petals form a tube with 5 flaring tips. Stamens and pistil extend beyond the flaring petal tips. A single pistil forms one dry fruit with the dried sepals (called the pappus).

Verbenaceae (Vervain)

Small, 4- or 5-part flowers in spikes or heads. Fused petals with 2 pairs of stamens attached.

Violaceae (Violet)

Flowers with 5 petals, a lower wide petal often extends back into a spur. Low growing herbaceous plants.

PTERIDOPHYTES
Non-flowering Vascular Plants
Ferns, Clubmosses and Horsetails

These plants have vessels (xylem and phloem) which conduct water and nutrients throughout the plant. The mode of reproduction differs because these plants do not produce fruit and seeds from flowers. Pteridophytes have spore-forming structures called sporangia; from these spores, a new plant life-cycle begins.

Equisetaceae (Horsetail)

Sporangia are located on top of ribbed, jointed stems. Non-green remnants of leaves form at the joints. Green stems carry out photosynthesis to nourish the plants. Curiously, the ribs take up silica, making them rough.

Lycopodiaceae (Clubmoss)

Mostly trailing plants. Upright branches have small, green leaves. Sporangia are found on special leaves at branch tips.

Ferns

Botrychiaceae (Moonwort)

This is a small family previously reported as being in *Ophioglossaceae.*

Dennstaedtiaceae (Bracken)

This is a new family name which includes ferns formerly in *Polypodiaceae. Dennstaedtiaceae* is now the largest family of ferns.

Dryopteridaceae (Wood Fern)

A large group of wood ferns are used as landscape plants including, Lady, Male, Leatherwood and Berry Bladder Ferns.

Ophioglossaceae (Succulent Ferns)

Ferns with soft, fleshy stems that have 1 (sometimes 2) leaves. Adder's-tongue, Grape and Rattlesnake Ferns are representative of this Family.

Osmundaceae (Flowering Ferns)

"Flowering" is a misnomer as no true flowers are formed. Rather, modified portions of fronds have spore cases which are conspicuous and may appear as withered flowers.

Polypodiaceae (Polypody)

Largest of the fern families, Polypody Ferns have spore cases on the underside of their fronds. These spores may be in dots over the surface or arranged along the margin of the fronds.

Pteridaceae (Maidenhair)

Maidenhair fern has been moved out of *Polypodiaceae.*

Bloomin' Season's Over!

Scientific Names

Common Names

Kings Creek Park ~ Duluth, Minnesota
A relaxing place for wildflower hunting!

Bibliography

Anderson, Allan. 1996. The reintroduction of Platanthera ciliaris in Canada. Proceedings, North American Native Orchid Conference.

Bailey, L. H. 1929. The standard encyclopedia of horticulture, vol. II. Macmillan.

Bates, J. 1995. Trailside Botany: 101 favorite trees, shrubs and wildflowers of the upper Midwest. Pfeifer-Hamilton.

Bennett, S. and T. Sullivan. 1999. Wildflower safaris by car. Arctic Riviera Publishing.

Black, M. R. and Emmet J. Judziewicz. 2009. Wildflowers of Wisconsin. University of Wisconsin Press.

Cobb, B. 1984. A field guide to ferns. Houghton Mifflin.

Cullina, William. 2000. Wildflowers: A Guide to Growing and Propagating Native Flowers of North America. (The New England Wild Flower Society). Houghton Mifflin.

Forey, P. 1991. Wildflowers of North America. W. H. Smith Publishers. Inc.

Gleason. H. A. and A. Cronquist. 1991. Manual of vascular plants of northeastern United States and adjacent Canada. 2nd ed. The New York Botanical Garden, Bronx, N.Y.

Harrington, H. D. 1977. How to identify grasses & grasslike plants. Swallow Press/University of Ohio Press.

Holmgren, N. H. 1998 . Illustrated companion to Gleason and Cronquist's manual: Illustrations of the vascular plants of northeastern United States and Adjacent Canada. The New York Botanical Garden.

Knobel, E. 1980. Field guide to the grasses, sedges and rushes of the United States. Dover Press.

Lakela, O. 1965. A flora of Northeastern Minnesota. University of Minnesota Press.

Lincoff, Gary H. 1981. National Audubon Society Field Guide to Mushrooms.

Loegering, W. Q. and E. P. DuCharme. 1978. Plants of the Canoe Country. Pfeifer-Hamilton.

Lund, H. C. 1998. Michigan wildflowers in color. Thunder Bay Press.

Mathis, William. 2005. The Gardener's Guide to Growing Hardy Perennial Orchid. The Wild Orchid Company.s

Moyle, J. B., and E. W., Moyle. 1977. Northland wildflowers. University of Minnesota Press.

Naegele, T. A. 1996. Edible and medicinal plants of the Great Lakes region. Wilderness Adventure Books, Davis, Michigan.

Newcomb, L. 1977. Newcomb's wildflower guide. Little Brown and Company.

Peterson, L. A. 1977. A field guide to edible wild plants of eastern and central North America. Houghton Mifflin.

Peterson, R. T. and M. McKenny. 1968. A field guide to wildflowers of northeastern and north-central North America. Houghton Mifflin.

Porter, C. L. 1967. Taxonomy of flowering plants, 2nd Ed. W. H. Freeman and Company.

Royer, F. and R. Dickinson. 1999. Weeds of the northern U. S. and Canada. The University of Alberta Press.

Smith, W. R. 2008. Trees and Shrubs of Minnesota. University of Minnesota Press.

Smith, W. R. 1993. Orchids of Minnesota. University of Minnesota Press.

Stensaas, Mark. 1996. Canoe country flora. Pfeifer-Hamilton.

Tekiela, S. 1999. Wildflowers of Minnesota. Adventure Publications.

Thayer, Samuel. 2006. The Forager's Harvest. Forager's Harvest.

Tullock, John.2005. Growing Hardy Orchids. Timber Press.

SOURCES OF NURSERY PROPAGATED NATIVE PLANTS

This list includes sources used by the author. There are other sources, but these have been found to furnish good quality plants. Check out native wild flowers on the web.

BOREAL NATIVES
www.prairieresto.com/boreal_natives.shtml
borealnatives@prairieresto.com
3943 Munger Shaw Road
Cloquet, MN 55720
218-729-7001

HICKORY ROAD GARDENS
brayherbs@msn.com
715-693-6446
2041 Hickory Road
Mosinee, WI 54455
Garden grown woodland species

DRAGONFLY GARDENS
491 State Hwy 46
P.O. Box 192, Amery, WI 54001
715-268-4666
www.dragonflygardens.net

HI-MOUNTAIN FARM
himtn@wildblue.net
Rt 1 Box 1425-A
Washburn, MO 65772

HILLSIDE NURSERY
www.hillsidenursery.biz
several species and selected cultivars.
A mail order only business

ITASCA LADYSLIPPER FARM
www.ladyslipperfarm.com
ladyslipperfarm@gmail.com
218-247-0245
14958 River Road,
Grand Rapids, MN 55744.
Container-grown, flowering size; from seedlings
produced by Spangle Creek Labs

KINNICKINNIC NATIVES
235 State Rd 65
River Falls, WI 54022
715-425-7605

LANDSCAPE ALTERNATIVES, Inc.
www.landscapealternatives.com
25316 St. Croix Trail
Shafer, MN 55074
651-257-4460
Retail and wholesale nursery

OUTBACK NURSERY
www.outbacknursery.com
15280 110th Street South
Hastings, MN. 55033
651-438-2771

PRAIRE MOON NURSERY
www.prairiemoon.com.
info@prairiemoon.com
866-417-8156
Native seeds and plants for praire, wetland, savanna and
woodland.

SPANGLE CREEK LABS.
www.spanglecreeklabs.com
ladyslippers@isp.com
218-247-0245
21950 County Road 445
Bovey, MN 55709
Lab-propagated seedlings of Cypripedium lady's-slippers; specializes in species native to eastern North
America.

SUNSHINE GARDENS
sunshinegardens.tripod.com
sgardens@uslink.net
1236 Shady Shores DR NW
Pine River, MN 56474
218-947-3154.

VERMONT LADYSLIPPER COMPANY
www.vtladyslipper.com
56 Leduc Road
New Haven, Vermont 05472-1000
802-877-2378
Specializing in the genus Cypripedium; laboratory
propagated from seed

WILD ORCHID COMPANY
www.wildorchidcompany.com
wildorchidco@earthlink.net
215-297-5403
215-297-0578 fax
Hardy Perennial Orchids
Also has a book on Growing Wild Orchids.

INFORMATION SOURCE

Wild Ones: Native Plants, Natural Landscapes, is a national non-profit based in Appleton, Wisconsin, that promotes landscaping with native plants through public education and advocacy.

Local Wild Ones chapters enjoy gathering together to learn from each other and featured speakers, exchange native plants or seeds, host local conferences and other public education events, or to organize plant rescues on construction sites. There are currently 46 Chapters of Wild Ones in 13 states. In addition, there are 36 more states with individual members. For more information on the Journal, chapters, benefits of Wild Ones membership and much more go to:

www.wildones.org or call 877-FYI-WILD.

Arctic Lupine *Lupinus arcticus*
Second place, wildflower category, in Wild One's photo contest 2009
photo taken in Denali National Park, Alaska by author

Last Minute Addition

Cloudberry
Rubus chamaemorus
Rosaceae **(Rose) Family**

Cloudberry is native only to the far northeastern counties of Minnesota in the upper Great Lakes region. However, it is common from Alaska to Eastern Canada, into the New England states and across Northern Europe and Asia. Fruit (see inset) is picked for jam and jelly in these regions.

Public Domain

Joshua Horky

About the Author

As you may suspect by reading Plant Names 101 on page xii, Clayton Oslund is a retired teacher. He taught High School Vocational Agriculture along with Biology and Chemistry for four years. Following further education (M.A. at University of Michigan), he taught at the University of Minnesota, Crookston campus. His final educational advancement was earning a Ph.D. in Horticulture (Plant Physiology) at the University of Minnesota. Teaching remained in his blood. The next 20 years were spent teaching Biology at the University of Minnesota's two year college in Waseca, Minnesota. This campus was dedicated to agricultural degrees.

Teaching continues to be paramount, however, in ways different from the traditional classroom setting. Clayton works extensively with Garden Clubs, Master Gardener groups, presents courses for "University for Seniors", consults, and writes.

He, along with his wife of times gone by, wrote the first edition of this book (*What's Doin' the Bloomin?*) and a travel guide, *Hawaiian Gardens are to Go To*. The travel guide to the gardens of Hawaii came about as a result of conducting a travel study course (Applied Tropical Botany) for 10 consecutive years with his university students while teaching at the Waseca campus. After retirement, Clayton conducted seven more non-university Hawaiian Garden tours.

As a thank you for purchasing this "Bloomin' book", I will mail an autographed copy of my Hawaiian Gardens guide book for $5.00 (cover price $19.95). For more details, look it up on Amazon.com for a "search inside".

If you take this book along on a trip to Hawaii, you will be glad you have it!

If you have already visited there, this book will make you want to go again to see all that you missed!!

Your request will reach me at:
P O Box 3224
Duluth, MN 55803

The state flower of Hawaii:
Native Yellow Hibiscus
Pua Aloalo; Ma`o hau hele.
Hibiscus brackenridgei
Malvaceae (Mallow) Family

Finally Done?

Winter Sunrise over Lake Superior